From Idolatress
to Child of God

From Where I Was to Where I Am Now!

Marjorie Kusi

Trilogy Christian Publishers
A Wholly Owned Subsidiary of Trinity Broadcasting Network
2442 Michelle Drive
Tustin, CA 92780

Copyright © 2024 by Marjorie Kusi

All Scripture quotations are taken from the ESV® Bible (The Holy Bible, English Standard Version®), copyright © 2001 by Crossway Bibles, a publishing ministry of Good News Publishers. Used by permission. All rights reserved.

All rights reserved, including the right to reproduce this book or portions thereof in any form whatsoever.

For information, address Trilogy Christian Publishing Rights Department, 2442 Michelle Drive, Tustin, CA 92780.

Trilogy Christian Publishing/ TBN and colophon are trademarks of Trinity Broadcasting Network.

For information about special discounts for bulk purchases, please contact Trilogy Christian Publishing.

Trilogy Disclaimer: The views and content expressed in this book are those of the author and may not necessarily reflect the views and doctrine of Trilogy Christian Publishing or the Trinity Broadcasting Network.

10 9 8 7 6 5 4 3 2 1

Library of Congress Cataloging-in-Publication Data is available.
ISBN 979-8-89333-121-9
ISBN 979-8-89333-122-6 (ebook)

TABLE OF CONTENTS

MY TESTIMONY 9

MY TESTIMONY 11

MY TESTIMONY 13

MY TESTIMONY 15

MY TESTIMONY 17

MY TESTIMONY 19

MY TESTIMONY 21

MY TESTIMONY 23

MY TESTIMONY 25

MY TESTIMONY 27

MY TESTIMONY 29

MY TESTIMONY 31

SACRIFICIAL CEREMONIAL 33

MY COMMITMENT WITH THE LORD 35

GOD'S LOVE FOR US 37

GOD'S LOVE FOR US 39

GOD'S LOVE FOR US 41

DO NOT CURSE ANYONE 43

JEHOVAH RAPHA THE HEALER 45

KNOWING HOLY GOD 47

DO NOT JUDGE THE ADDICTS 49

STRONG FAITH 51

SPOUSES WHO DO NOT KNOW
HOW TO LOVE EACH OTHER. 53

DO NOT BE A ROUGH STONE 55

WALKING WITH GOD. 57

WALKING WITH GOD
THROUGH THE DARK TIME 59

GREAT RELATIONSHIP WITH GOD. 61

DEALING WITH TEMPTATION 63

POWERFUL PRACTICE OF FASTING 65

BENEFITS OF FASTING. 67

WHY DO NOT WE LISTEN TO GOD?. 69

WAYS TO SHOW ENCOURAGEMENT. 71

WHEN WE ARE REALLY IN NEED
OF SOMETHING IMPORTANT 73

TRUSTING IN GOD 75

WHAT IS GOD'S PURPOSE?. 77

WHAT DOES GOD WANT? 79

FILLED WITH THE HOLY SPIRIT 81

GUIDED BY THE HOLY SPIRIT 83

GUIDED BY THE HOLY SPIRIT 85

GUIDED BY THE HOLY SPIRIT 87

THE HOLY SPIRIT: AN ABSOLUTE ESSENTIAL 89

THE CHARACTERISTICS OF GOD 91

GOD'S MERCY 93

PAY ATTENTION WHEN PRAYING
WITH PEOPLE OVER THE PHONE 95

PAY ATTENTION WHEN PRAYING
WITH PEOPLE OVER THE PHONE 97

DIED IN OURSELVES 99

HOW GOD GETS OUR ATTENTION. 101

TITHES AND OFFERINGS 103

TITHES AND OFFERINGS 105

TITHES AND OFFERINGS 107

ASKING, SEARCHING, AND KNOCKING 109

ASKING, SEARCHING, AND KNOCKING 111

WE MUST KNOW WHO WE ARE 113

WE MUST KNOW WHO WE ARE 115

CAUGHT UP IN A BAD SITUATION
AS BELIEVERS. 117

CAUGHT UP IN A BAD SITUATION
AS BELIEVERS. 119

CAUGHT UP IN A BAD SITUATION
AS BELIEVERS. 121

MY HOPE TO HEAVEN 123

MY HOPE TO HEAVEN 125

MY HOPE TO HEAVEN 127

LET DOWN OUR PRIDE. 129

LET DOWN OUR PRIDE. 131

THE THREE ANGELS' MESSAGES 133

THE THREE ANGELS' MESSAGES 135

THE THREE ANGELS' MESSAGES 137

GOD'S GOODNESS 141

GOD'S GOODNESS 143

PRISON MINISTRY OR EVANGELIST 145

PRISON MINISTRY OR EVANGELIST 147

WHERE ARE WE SPIRITUALLY? 149

WHERE ARE WE SPIRITUALLY? 151

WHERE ARE WE SPIRITUALLY? 153

WHERE ARE WE SPIRITUALLY? 155

WHERE ARE WE SPIRITUALLY? 157

WHERE ARE WE SPIRITUALLY? 159

WHERE ARE WE SPIRITUALLY? 161

FAMILY 163

FAMILY 165

FAMILY 167

LEARN TO SERVE OTHERS 169

LEARN TO SERVE OTHERS 171

My Testimony

MY TESTIMONY

In the spring of 2014, someone I had met at a friend's house was in the neighborhood that I used to live in. She invited me to a revival at her church. I did not mind that she had someone in the passenger seat, and I did not know that it was one of her church members. I said to her, "Look who is talking about revival! Aren't you the one I always saw when I go to parties? Aren't you the one that I used to see at the train station going to New York for the Labor Day Weekend?"

She did not answer me, but she gave me the flyer that had all the information about the revival.

I told her if it were someone else that invited me, I would have gone, but she could not talk to me about neither Christ nor revival. Even though I took the flyer from her, I did not go to the revival.

I could not believe that next spring of 2015, exactly a year since she invited me to that revival, I met with her again! I met her at the same parking lot where she invited me before. She said, "As you can see, I just dropped my friend off, and I saw you right where I met you last year. This time I will not take no for an answer."

In my heart, I felt like she would not leave me alone. Then I asked her, "Are you crazy? What is wrong with you? You came last year, and I chased you away! And now you are back."

She said, "I did not have to drive; she would pick me up every single day."

I told her, "Last year at this time, in this very month, you came to bother me. You do not have anything to do."

She did not answer. Then I asked her what she wanted from me. She said, "I want to invite you to this year's revival that will take place at my church."

I told her, "If I were you, I would look for something else to do."

She said, "That's what I should do, by inviting you to go to church with me."

Then I asked her if she did not have friends or co-workers.

MY TESTIMONY

She answered, "You do not have to be someone's friend to offer them Jesus Christ or to share the gospel with them."

I told her that I was not ready for what she was talking about.

Even at that time, it had been five months since I had prayed to the Almighty, asking Him if He wanted me to repent and to watch over my kids so what I used to serve and worship did not follow my kids.

Even when I felt like I was not ready to accept Jesus of Nazareth in my life, I prayed to Him. He did not reject my prayers for the five months that I asked Him to protect my children and me.

Repentance is something that I did not have in mind and did not see coming. That woman insisted she pick me up to go to the revival because I did not go in the previous year after she invited me.

I wanted her to leave me alone, but that was not what happened. Then she said that she would not trust me, because of last time when I realized she would not take no for an answer. Then I gave up.

I said, "Yes, I will go," but I knew I was not going anywhere. I told her I would go by myself, and she did not believe me.

She wanted to pick me up, and I said, "Okay, you can come to get me."

She said she would be there every day to pick me up to go to her church, but there was a problem, because I did not have church clothes to wear. Although I was not a Christian, I knew I could not go to church with the kind of clothes that I used to wear.

From that afternoon, when I finally agreed to go to that revival, I started going to the store to buy casual clothes to wear for the first week. I did the same for the second and third week until the revival was over.

The first day of that revival was May 9th, 2015. I was there from that day, until the day that I had born again. The night of May 9th, I had a dream, where I saw myself in the church that I was in that morning.

MY TESTIMONY

I saw myself in the suit pants that I wore for the first day of that revival. Remember, I did not have church clothes, but I used to wear suit pants to go to funerals. I thought I had to impress people on the first day of my invitation! So, I dressed in one of my suit pants.

After I saw myself the way I was that day, I heard a very loud voice the same way God had called Moses in the burning bush. That voice had called me in my birth name that I did not give at the church.

No one knew my birth name at that church; even the lady that invited me did not know my birth name. The name that I heard from the loud voice that called me in my dream that night, was not the one that I wrote on the guest list.

In that dream I saw myself seated where I was in the morning, and the church was very still; no sound and no activities at all. That was when I heard an extraordinarily strong voice calling my birth name from the right side of the church.

I was shocked, because I did not know who could know my name like that over there. Nobody knew my name at the church. I got up anyway, I walked up to the right side of the church looking for who called my name.

While I walked to the right side, I heard the same loud

voice calling my birth name for a second time, but that time it was on the left side of the church.

I made my way to the left side of the church. As soon as I started to walk to the left side of the church, I heard that same voice even louder calling my birth name for the third time in front of the altar.

In my dream, I saw myself standing between two men in front of the whole church. Those two men dressed like royal guards. They had on a kilt from their waist to above the knees, and their chests were naked.

I had one guard on my left side with a spear in his left hand. There was another guard on my right side with a spear in his right hand. When I had met the trials and temptations, I realized that God had already had me before I was even born again. The God of Israel that was calling my name in that church to leave the world that was leave in.

MY TESTIMONY

While I was in between those two men in front of the altar, where I was facing the church members and the visitors, I realized that the King of kings wanted me to be one of His servants and one of His followers.

When I woke up from that dream, I was thinking, and I found out, it was God that was watching over me all my life. Those were not the idols that my parents and I were serving. Then I questioned myself, *what kind of God is He?*

Even when I did not know Him, I was not a Christian. He was looking for me to turn my life around; I could not wait for the morning to call that lady who invited me to that revival so I could tell her about my dream.

Like I said, I started going there on May 9th, and on May 12th I surrendered my life to Jesus Christ. That I did not see coming because I was not ready for that.

After, I heard the preacher say people were dying by a lack of knowledge. Then he mentioned that most people thought they could sin all they wanted, because if they couldn't make it to Heaven after their death, they would go to purgatory to purify themselves there to be able to go to Heaven.

I heard the preacher say there is no such thing as purgatory in the Bible, there is Heaven or Hell. He said the purgatory is the devil's way to take people to hell with him as the father of all lies.

I could not believe what I heard, because that was what my parents knew. That was what we believed in. My parents and I did not know the truth. When I heard that from the preacher, it was painful to know that my ancestors and my parents were going to hell for what they had believed in.

From that day, which was May 12th, 2015, I surrendered my life completely to God. My parents and I thought that the only hope to take us to Heaven was purgatory, but that was not true.

MY TESTIMONY

I found out the truth that the devil did not want me to know. The only hope to take me to Heaven was a great and sincere relationship with Jesus Christ. After I raised my right hand to accept Christ, the secretary of that church came to me and asked me what my name was to add it in the candidates' baptismal list.

On my first day at the revival, I gave my married name. Yet the Creator knew me than anyone else; He used my birth name to call me, so I had no choice but to give the church secretary my birth name.

The day after I gave my name to the secretary, I started gathering everything that I was not supposed to deal with anymore, things like CDs, DVDs, roseries. The idols so-called saints in woods, in irons, in rocks, and in plastics.

Anything that could make me look back to where I was, that I was not supposed to have at my house nor in my car anymore, was packed to throw away.

I was not a Christian, but I knew if I wanted to be a faithful one, I had to let go of the past even if I thought I was not ready to be a Christian yet. I knew if I did not let go of the past there would not be any transition in my life.

It took me a week to clean that mess that I was in. Everyday when I made it home from work, the first thing I had to do was to carry stuff out to trash until I was done taking those things out of my place. I did not want for the pastor and the elders who were supposed to come to pray with me before I got baptized to see that mess.

It was true I was blind, but as soon as I could see what mess that I was in, I had to clean that mess. Those idols were things that I had collected for years! I did not want to be embarrassed so I cleaned my place before they came.

When they had come to pray for me, I felt exceptionally light, because my house was free from idols that I used to worship because I did not know better.

MY TESTIMONY

If my parents and I knew then what I found out in 2015, I am sure they would have had a place waiting for them like me in Heaven.

Unbelievably, on May 20th, 2015, I was born again and became a child of God. I do not have to be afraid anymore. I am not a slave of sins anymore; my toes will not hurt from working the world that I used to be in anymore.

I am not a slave of idols anymore; I am not painting sins anymore. When I went in the water to get baptized, I was dead with Jesus Christ. When I stood up in the water, all my sins washed away.

I thank God for that invitation, because now I am free from being a slave of idols, things that God does not like. Now that I am free because Jesus Christ paid my debt in full for me. I am not worthy to even say His Holy name, but He is my Savior.

The very night that I was born again, I asked God to put His strengths in my weakness so I could be strong to serve Him faithfully until the day of His return.

Right after I became born again, I found out about storms, challenges, persecutions, and temptations. Just when I got away from the storms, the challenges showed up. When I thought challenges were over, persecutions showed up; when I thought persecutions were over, trials and temptations showed up.

That family member who was my mentor had told me, "Now you have been evaluated, either by God Almighty or by the devil."

If after I became a Christian, I had not asked the Almighty to give me His strengths, I would be in my grave right now. The persecutions, the storms, and the challenges were very intense.

I cannot thank Jesus of Nazareth enough! Because He did not let any devil agents discourage me nor let me think of going back when I told my mentor about what was going on in church. Before I was born again, I thought everybody in church were spiritual.

MY TESTIMONY

My mentor said, "Why don't you look what Matthew 7: 21-23 says?"

> *Not everyone who says to me, "Lord" will enter the kingdom of heaven, but the one who does the will of my Father who is in heaven. On that day many will say to me, "Lord, Lord, did we not prophesy in your name, and do many mighty works in your name?" And then I will declare to them, "I never knew you; depart from me, you workers of lawlessness."*
>
> **–Matthew 7:21-23**

This is a reminder to always keep in mind the one and only model that I will always have is Jesus Christ, my Savior.

I ask God to always keep me under His wings and His garments, so I can be the Christian He wants me to be. I know nobody is perfect, but I always seek His help, and I try to stay obedient to Him and listen to Him.

My mentor told me to always keep my eyes on Jesus Christ. No matter what happened, that family member was a great mentor for me.

I thank God for that family member who was a mentor to me, who had told me to watch my steps, because I could not walk in the dark anymore. He told me that I was a new person, I should walk like it and act like it sincerely.

He had reminded me this two times so I would not forget that after Jesus Christ, no one could be my model, no family members, friends, co-workers, or church members.

I thank God for that lady that invited me to that revival as well.

> *You are the salt of the earth, but if the salt has lost its taste, how shall its saltiness be restored? It is no longer good for anything except to be thrown out and trampled under peoples' feet. You are the light of the world. A city set on a hill cannot be hidden. Nor do people light a lamp and put it under a basket, but on a stand, and it gives light to all in the house. In the same way, let your light shine before others so they may see your good works and give glory to your Father who is in heaven.*
>
> **–Matthew 5:13-16, ESV**

Then he said, "I do not just say things to you; but I gave you references so you can see what I told you is in the Bible." After listening to him and reading what he had sent me to read, I felt extraordinarily strong.

MY TESTIMONY

From that day, until the day I die, I will always keep my word to follow Jesus of Nazareth, my Redeemer and Savior, because I will always ask God to give me strength to be humble and sincerely faithful to Him for the rest of my life.

My family member/mentor told me to always stay in prayer, to never think of putting my trust in friends nor families because they could leave my side anytime. Jesus Christ would never leave my side.

Then He said to me, "Even me! I am not your model." Then he asked me to look for Joshua 1:9 (ESV): God says to Joshua, "Have I not commanded you? Be strong and courageous. Do not be frightened, and do not be dismayed, for the Lord your God is with you wherever you go."

He is the one who told me about God as a Promise Keeper. Then he had told me to keep on following Jesus Christ's footsteps sincerely, because when you are sincere with God, He promotes your strength to another dimension.

Just as a good listener, I listened to everything he had to say to me. He told me to always humble myself before God. I asked him, "what does the word humble mean, because I have heard you say that over and over." He said that means to always go on my knees when I am going to pray, because God is holy.

Following his instructions was the best thing that ever happened to me. He told me to pray whenever I feel like it and not wait for when I am in need to go to God. My mentor told me that I must make prayer my best friend, and that will be the best thing to help me build my relationship with God.

To have our minds always on the things of God, to be in constant communication with Him, makes it so that every moment may be as fruitful as possible. (1 Thessalonians 5:17.)

It is true that by staying in prayers with the grace of God, I overcame all the challenges, all the trials and temptations that I accounted for two years after I was born again.

I used to ask God if He wanted me to go to another church to let me know where to go. I never got any answer from Him. I visited other churches, but I stayed where He had called my name like I said before.

MY TESTIMONY

I thank God that He had called me, to leave the world that I knew with everything in it. Sometimes I ask myself, *What took me so long to get to know God? What was I waiting for to have Jesus Christ in my life?*

Now I can say that I have God because I have Him in my life. The dirt of the world will not get in my eyes anymore. What a grace! I found in God a second chance.

The first chance I got I blew it. He had sent for me again; until I can say, "What then shall we say to these things? If God is for us, who can be against us?" (Romans 8:31, ESV).

Whenever I remember how I used to be, where I used to be, I must give glory to God for what He has done for me. From where I was to where I am now! To where I am going.

My Savior raised me up from the dust and lifted me out of the dunghill; the Lord washed me with His blood, He put me in a clean place. He knew that I was a slave of sins, He forgave me for all I had done when I surrendered my life to Him.

Now, I know that I was in a dark place, for the times I had wasted before I met Jesus Christ. I wish I could get those times back to use them to preach the gospel instead of wasting my time.

I want to talk to people about Jesus of Nazareth. He had left His throne, just to show us how to serve His Father. For us He died on the cross. He resurrected, and He is coming back again.

My life changed after I met Jesus Christ. Let me tell you back then how my life used to be. I used to party with my only son, who was five years old. When I used to go to parties with him, I used to put his feet on top of mine so I could show him how to dance.

For him to be able to dance with my friends, I really did not know what I was doing to that kid. When they used to invite me to parties, we used to sleep early so we could wake up by ten at night and prepare ourselves to go to the parties.

MY TESTIMONY

I used to go to New York on the Friday of Labor Day Weekend, because I could not miss anything that was going on from that carnival.

Most of the time my family members that lived in New York knew that I was in the city for Labor Day, but I would not see them, because I was busy partying with my friends who lived in New York until the carnival was over.

On Tuesday morning I went back to New Jersey to go to work. I used to do whatever I wanted, whenever I wanted to. I used to go wherever I wanted whenever I wanted to.

After I met Jesus Christ, things changed.

I know that I must watch what I am doing. I cannot do whatever I please anymore, because God is holy, and He is omnipresent. This means He is everywhere.

It is true the past is gone, but I will always remember and tell the world where Jesus Christ had found me. He saved me to make me who I am today! A new person.

I thank God for His mercy that endures forever now that God woke me up from the dead. I am not a slave of idols anymore; I am not a slave of the world anymore; I will never be a slave of fear again.

The world will not give me toothache anymore. Leaving

with fear was what I was worried about. Now I know that I do not owe anybody; I am free today. Jesus Christ paid my dept in full of His blood.

I was born in an idol-worshipper family, which was all I ever knew. I grew up worshiping idols with my grandmother. We did not know that we were blind, we did not know better, because we did not have Jesus of Nazareth in our lives. So, we did not have the truth.

In my family, even we were idol worshippers. We had to have our first communion when we were little. Our parents used to tell us, "Do not say tomorrow, next week, next month, or next year without saying if God wants to." I know my God already forgives me because I did not know what I was doing.

The idols are not controlling my mind anymore. Jesus of Nazareth is controlling my mind and my life. Amen to that! With Jesus of Nazareth, I am free from idols and bondages today!

MY TESTIMONY

Now I realize, what they used to tell us did not mean anything because we did not have God in our lives. So, there is no way if we do not make it right with God while we are alive that we will make it to heaven by going to purgatory.

Prepare ourselves so we can go to heaven. Instead of worshiping the Creator, we used to worship the creations. Me personally, I did not know that I had to worship the Creator.

My parents and I knew that God is the Creator of everything, but we did not have Him in our lives, and I did not know that God gives us choice. I just knew what I had to do was to serve the idols. We did not know Him as our Father. If I have knew then what I know now, I would have been a child of God a long time ago.

My parents heard the gospel, but they just did not get it. They did not have all the information about it. The reason I said they did not get all the information was because we believed in purgatory. We used to believe if we could not go straight to heaven when we died it would be okay, because we would go to purgatory to prepare ourselves to go to heaven. I thank God for not letting me die without repentance. Thank God for His forgiveness, I will always remember where I was. To not go there anymore.

I believe God Almighty is everything that I ever needed. If I did not have God in my life today, I do not know what I would do. I wake up in the morning Jesus of Nazareth. When I am at work, there is Jesus of Nazareth. Everywhere I go to is Jesus of Nazareth. It is a name above all names. Nothing can come against that Holy name.

Sometimes, I ask myself why Holy God loves me like that? I know His love is without limit to save a sinner like me. I know I will never be able to thank Him enough for all the things He has done for me and my children. I did not know that God is a very jealous God. I had no one to tell me that God hates idols. I asked God for forgiveness through His only Son Jesus of Nazareth. I know that God is my Father, because He says in Micah 7:19 (ESV), He will again have compassion on us; he will tread our iniquities underfoot. You will cast all our sins into the depths of the sea." My life is a testimony of God's goodness. All the glory is to God. I will always be magnifying the Lord to proceed how big that He is.

I thank my God for His without limit love, for His compassion, for His mercy, for His grace and faithfulness. Who am I to call myself a child of God today?

SACRIFICIAL CEREMONIAL

I remember that I used to save money every year especially for the gods' sacrificial ceremony. Sometimes I did not have money to do important things for myself or my family, but I thought that I had to save money for the sacrificial ceremony that I had to do every summertime.

I had to buy a bull, a young heifer, a rooster, a chicken, a male and a female dove, a male and a female goat, a male and a female pig, a male and a female sheep.

I would have money to feed at least one hundred people and drinks to serve more than one hundred people. People did not really need to eat but came to drink alcohol so they could enjoy themselves. At that time, I did not realize that was a waste of money I did not have, but I was happy they came to dance and sing for the sacrificial ceremony.

It cost money to rent chairs for the twenty-one days of the sacrificial ceremonial services. From early morning to after midnight there should be things for them to drink. That did not bother me because it was my pleasure to give them what they needed at that time.

When we were little, we could not wait for school to be over so we could go to the the countryside that my grandmother came from to have fun there by participating in the sacrificial ceremony. It was a pleasure to us all we could not wait to go.

Fun! That was what we as children thought it was. They taught us to have respect for the gods. Which meant we needed to serve the gods the way they wanted to be served. I had to pay people especially to play music in that place. I also had to pay people to cook for the gods. I had to pay drummers to play from the day the sacrificial ceremony started to the day it ended.

On the last day of the sacrificial ceremonial, I had to pay another group of people to play a violin for the gods before I could call it quits.

My ancestors and I were so blind! We could not see and understand that the idols "have mouths, but do not speak; eyes, but do not see. They have ears, but do not hear; noses, but do not smell. They have hands, but do not feel; feet, but do not walk; and they do not make a sound in their throat. Those who make them become like them; so do all who trust in them." (Psalms 115:5-8, ESV).

I did not know the day that Jesus of Nazareth sacrificed His precious life on the cross for my sins, that sacrificial ceremony was over. I was in the world like I said; I did not know better. Matthew 27:51 (ESV) says, "And be hold, the curtain of the temple was torn in two, from top to bottom. And the earth shook, and the rocks were split."

If I knew then what I know now! I would never have wasted my time and money on those things.

MY COMMITMENT WITH THE LORD

Since the day I was born again, I have asked God to please give me the strength that I will need to follow Him sincerely and faithfully, serving Him until the day I die. I will always keep my word to follow Jesus of Nazareth, my Redeemer and Savior, because I always ask God to give me strength to be humble and truthfully keep my covenant with Him.

My family member/mentor told me to always stay in communion, and in prayer, with the Lord. Never to think of putting my trust in friends nor families because they could leave my side anytime, but Jesus of Nazareth would never leave my side.

Then he said, "Even me! That baptized when I was ten years old; I am not your model." That mentor was the one who told me to keep follow Jesus of Nazareth's footsteps until the day I die. He told me, "When you are sincere with God, He will let you know everything that is coming in your way, good or bad."

Just as a good listener, I listened to everything he had to say to me. He told me to always humble myself before God. Don't think that I can live without God, not even for one minute in my life. I was told by him to always go on my knees when I prayed, because God lifted the humble.

I followed his instructions, which were the best things to ever happen to me. He told me to pray whenever I felt like it and not to wait for when I need something to go to God. He told me to read the Bible every single day. He said if I read three pages of the Bible every day from January 1st to December 31st, I will have read all the sixty-six books in the Bible. Since that day, I knew that I must pray and give glory to God in good and bad times, and I read the words that could help me build my relationship with the Lord and did just that.

By staying in communion with the Lord, He helped me overcame all the challenges. All the trials and temptations that I accounted for two years after I was born again. I used to ask God if He wanted me to go to another church to let me know where to go. I never received any answers from Him. I visited other churches, but I stayed where He had called my name like in that dream that I was talking about at the beginning.

GOD'S LOVE FOR US

I am not worthy to say His holy name, but my God, my Father, and my best friend forever saved me. I did not know I was that valuable, that a costly ransom of infinite price was paid for me.

I am not worthy to say Jesus of Nazareth's name, while My Lord and Savior, my adoptive brother, takes me from idol slavery. I am not worthy of His grace and forgiveness, but He forgives me anyway.

What a formidable God He is; everybody has their own god, but we as Christians have the true God. He is trustworthy, unfailing, constant and steadfast; that is the kind of God that we are serving.

He never forgets, never falters, and never fails to keep His word. He is truthful about every aspect, He will never mislead us, He sees in the darkness because He is the great light.

We cannot hide anything from Him. He knows everything about us even before our existence because He is our Creator. God is everything we ever need in our lives.

As Jesus Christ followers, we need to love everyone, even people who do not want to be loved. Jesus Christ does not choose who to love, He loves everybody.

Since He commands us to love one another, the best thing to do is to be a good listener. We need to try our best to learn to love like Jesus our Savior.

We are not talking about sentimental love; we are talking about love sacrificially. Which means to give of ourselves to others. Sacrificial love also means loving unconditional. The important thing is not to choose who to love, because our Savior did not choose who to love. He sacrificed Himself as a part of all genuine love for us. His love is without limits. Love is patient, instead of anger and discontent. The only one that can love us as we deserved to be loved is God.

As a father shows compassion to his children, so the Lord shows compassion to those who fear Him.

–Psalm 103:13

GOD'S LOVE FOR US

We can look for love from a relationship, but we will never find it. Whatever you do wrong in a relationship, before you know it, the relationship will be over. God's love is unconditional, nobody can love us like God loves us. If we choose protection, we are going to be disappointed. God's love is the only one that is going to make us content and happy for the rest of our lives.

When we sin against God, He does not cut ties with us, He does not unbid with us. He gives us Jesus Christ, so we can ask Him for forgiveness for our sins.

Even the devil always tries to make us think that we can sin and get away with it. The devil's work is to make us keep on sinning and makes us feel ashamed. Shame is not come from the Lord; it comes from the devil. God loves the sinner, but He hates the sin.

We need to act like God, to not hate people for what they look like or what they have done, but to love them for who they are. Jesus Christ followers or not. We just need to pray for them so their eyes can open, and they will have a better understanding of what a Christian's life is about.

God loves us for who we are not for what society want us to be. We do not have to kill ourselves or try to change ourselves to be good enough for anyone. Remember that we will never be good enough for anybody.

The change that we need to make is when we accept Jesus Christ as our Savior and Lord. We let go of our past and move forward, let God make the changes that He sees that we will need so we can serve Him better.

We are too smart to let the devil continue getting in our head to do what is not right to please him, and to displease our Lord. The devil knows that his time is no more, but God knows the devil's plans are to make us deceive Him. That is why God gives us Jesus Christ to go to, when we want and need to ask for forgiveness.

> *Do not love the world or anything in the world. If anyone loves the world, love for the father is not in them.*

–1 John 2:15

GOD'S LOVE FOR US

If there one thing that we think we really need to do or want to do, it is to love everyone. It does not have to be our best friends or our family member. We must love one another for God's sake. We do not know how life without love is a miserable life. As Christians, we must feel love every single day, love must be what we do best for people. Believers should love everyone without falling in love with unbelievers. Love should be in our hearts every single day.

We can give everything we own to the world if we do not have love; we do not have anything. If we do not have love for the Lord, we will not have love for anybody else. We must have love for the Lord to have love for other people.

Love is time! Time means love. We must be patient to love because love at first sight is not going to be everywhere we go. The same way there are people that do not believe in love at first sight. That is the same way there are people that are so difficult to love. Nothing can replace time, but hatred can be replaced by love. We already know that we should not have a place for hatred in our hearts.

We must ask God to give us the courage that we need to not keep a place in our hearts for hatred and other things that can push away the Holy Spirit. Our hearts must stay clean for the Holy Spirit to live in it.

We need to fulfill our purpose here on earth by following Jesus Christ, preaching the gospel, and helping others. Same way we would want others to help us. When we start changing the way we used to do things our way in our own time or when we felt like it instead of leaving things to God. When we think about what is good for others no matter who they are, Christians or unbelievers, when we stop being selfish and die in ourselves, finally, we will say that we are Christ-like.

We must stop saying things to make people feel good, things to make people feel happy. We were not called to gain fans but to make discipleship. We need to ask God to change us from who we are now, to mold us to whom He wants us to be. We all know that cannot happen overnight for us, but God is the Creator of the universe. He can make that happen in a blank of an eye because everything is possible with Him.

> *Call on me and I will answer you and tell you great and unsearchable things you do not know.*
>
> **–Jeremiah 33:3**

DO NOT CURSE ANYONE

In the year of 2016, one year after I was born again, someone did me wrong. I was so mad, I did not only wish bad things for that person, but I also asked God to take care of that person for me. Since I knew I was a Christian, I did not have to argue or fight with that person.

I went on my knees to ask God to send a storm to that person, because I heard whatever problem we had as Christians, the only thing we could do was to go to God.

Every day when I prayed, I never forgot to ask God to give me justice for the pain and suffering that I had to go through. To me it was okay to ask God for justice because people always say that the Lord is a God of justice.

So, I asked God to make that person pay for what I went through. I thought I did what I was supposed to do, go to my Father to complain to Him about who did me wrong, and then things would be all right.

But it did not work that way. God showed me what was about to happen in my dream. When I woke up in the morning, I went on my knees and asked God, "What do You want to say to me? I do not understand what is going on."

Then I said, "Please! Help me understand what is about to happen to me."

43

Later that night, I had a dream where I was singing a baptism ceremonial song. When I woke up, I opened my hymnal book, and I started learning the song that I was singing in my dream. I was questioning myself, *why did I see me singing that song?*

Oh my God! That dream troubled me for days because the song is about repentance. I asked myself, *why this song?* I could not understand that I did anything wrong to ask God for forgiveness, because I just asked Him for justice.

Two months later the storm that I had asked God to send to that person came my way. Troubles and all the rest. I never discouraged of praying. I would pray in the morning when I woke up, I always did my midday prayer and midnight prayer.

You will not believe that it took two years for the storm to go away. It was God's way to show me that a true Christian should not ask for bad to happen to anybody but only pray for whoever can be changed.

JEHOVAH RAPHA THE HEALER

I thank Jehovah Rapha for His healing business, otherwise I would not be here today. One year after I was born again, I had a storm that I prayed God to send to someone who was hurting me so badly, as I told you before.

I thought it was fine to do but, God wanted to show me a true Christian should not wish dreadful things to anyone whatsoever. That storm was poison, everything that I touched contaminated.

Whatever it was, sheets, pillowcases, blankets, dresses, even finger food. When I said everything, I meant everything under the sun. Finger foods were the worst ever because I would forget to wear gloves before I put anything in my mouth.

Even curtains, tablecloths, chairs, living room seats cushions, remote controls. I could not touch myself without gloves otherwise I would scream, this poison was the worst storm I had ever known in my entire life.

The private parts in my body were the easiest to get contaminated. I had to wear gloves to brush my teeth, to cook and wash dishes. To wash myself, to take showers, to put clothes on. If I forget to wear gloves, I was in big trouble.

If I wore my clothes without wearing a pair of gloves, it

was important for me.

Even after six months or a year, when I put those clothes back on, I had to take them off fast because the poison was still there.

I had to throw away everything that I touched without gloves, because I was not able to touch or use them ever again. It took over two years to suffer with that storm. I called it a storm because that was what I had prayed to happened to someone.

God let that poison stress me out for so long to change my behavior. So, I know what storms are like to never ask anything bad to happen to anyone ever again.

I have learned to never act that way ever again. I could die from that poison because I had never had any pain, any discomfort. One day I went to the bathroom, and I saw lots of cancer cells full of fluids in the toilet bowl. I did not feel sick then until that day. I did not have to take chemotherapy nor radiation, because Jehovah Rapha the Healer healed me from 2016 to 2018. I thank the Medicator of medicators for my healing.

KNOWING HOLY GOD

Our God is holy, we must serve Him the way He wants us to serve Him, it is true we are not perfect, we are not holy, but we can serve Him right if we choose to by His strength.

As mothers we always say we are the only person in our children's lives that can give them the love they deserve. Our love will never compare to the love of the Almighty God.

Even if we did what is not right in the eyes of God, He still loves us. Sometimes we might account for too many problems, and temptations; usually we say these are too much to manage.

God never gives us what we cannot manage. Matthew 11: 28-30 (ESV) says, "Come to me, all who labor and are heavy laden, and I will give you rest. Take my yoke upon you, and learn from me, for I am gentle and lowly in heart, and you will find rest for your souls. For my yoke is easy, and my burden is light."

When we do not know what to do, God tells us what we are supposed to do. When we do not see why or how we are going to make it, by the grace of God, He makes a way to make it happen when there seems to be no way.

The best thing we must do as Christians is to lean on Jesus Christ our Savior. We will always be safer with Him. It is true we cannot be perfect, but we can ask God, "Please help me do better."

We can ask Jesus Christ our Lord and Savior to help us follow His footsteps. We can also ask Him to guide our spiritual lives. Knowing holy God isn't the same thing as saying, "I know about God." There is an enormous difference between knowing the Holy God and having the Holy God in our lives. When we have the Holy God in our lives, He has control over our lives and everything else. We do not have to worry about anything whatsoever.

DO NOT JUDGE THE ADDICTS

People like to judge other people because of their addictions. What they do not understand is that not everyone knows how to cope with challenges. For other people, alcohol is the only solution that can satisfy them.

Often the people that use alcohol do not want to use it but, for them, using alcohol is what can satisfy their souls. Same thing for people who use drugs, which is not what they want to do, but they think if they take drugs to sweep their problems under the mat, that can fill the emptiness they have. But will they be satisfied? They think that way because they are confused. I do not think addictions is what they are choosing to be. What about people that think they must use sleeping pills to sleep and pills to stay up; that is still an addiction.

When people take drugs and overdose, they end up killing themselves. You think that is what they want to do; I do not think so, and I think the devil made them dangerous to themselves and to people around them. No matter what they have tried they could not find what they were looking for, unless someone offered them Jesus Christ as their Savior or if they had turned to a Christian TV channel and heard about Jesus Christ who loves them and died for them.

They are looking for some things that can make them forget the situation that they are in. Most of the time people become food addicted. It is because when they are stressed the only thing that can help them feel better is eating. They do not have anyone that they can trust with their problems. Whatever the reason might be, they are stressed out and feel alone in the world that they are in. Who knows, they do not have someone to talk to about what troubled them, or anybody to care for them. They could find help if they wanted to go to therapy, but they think going to therapy is to give information to someone who will not be able to help them, but instead judge them or talk about them. Whatever they have tried did not work or satisfy them, that is why they have killed themselves. But if they were willing to accept Jesus of Nazareth as their Lord and Savior, their emptiness would be fulfilled.

Judge not, that you be not judged.

–Matthew 7:1

STRONG FAITH

To have a strong faith we must ask the Almighty God for His help so we can keep the faith that we have asked Him for. We can have a strong faith and a weak body; if we ask God for His strength we can always have a strong faith and strong body.

> *For truly I tell you, if you have faith the size of mustard seed, you will say to this mountain, 'Move from here to there,' and it will move; and nothing will be impossible for you.*
>
> **–Matthew 17:20**

When you place your faith in God you do not have to worry about anything, because the Almighty God has you. We do not have to count on our intelligence or our families and friends, with Him we are complete. That is what we all as Christians we need, to be satisfied by our Savior. Our Savior tells us to not worry about tomorrow. Matthew 6:34 says, "Therefore do not worry about tomorrow, for tomorrow will worry about itself. Each day has enough trouble of its own." This is part of the sermon of the Mount.

Strong faith makes us understand and learn to leave all to God, it shows us that we cannot leave without Him in our lives because, we should count only on Christ our Lord. We must always lean on God, because He is the only one who knows what is good for us. It is true sometimes what we want, that is what we think we are supposed to have.

The Lord always makes the best choice for us. His choice may not meet our expectations, but His choices are always the best for our lives. I cannot count all His choices, but His choices are great!

He wants us to be sincere with Him, He wants us to follow His right path, He wants us to love one another as He loves us no matter what we have done that is unpleasant to Him. He wants us to do the same for people that hurt us.

He wants us to serve Him and only Him. He wants us to give Him glory that He deserves. He wants us to forgive anyone that hurts us if we want Him to forgive us. He wants us to have a great relationship with Him and to keep the faith until the end of our lives. Jesus says when we are faithful in a little thing, He will trust us with a big thing. Do we have the faith the lady that was sick for twelve years had?

SPOUSES WHO DO NOT KNOW HOW TO LOVE EACH OTHER

Usually, people who complain about their spouses do not give them the attention that they deserve. If it is not the wife, it is the husband that always complains about what he or she does not do. That is not only for unbelievers, but also Christian lives too. Sometimes the one that expect more of his or her spouse does not even take time to ask questions. He or she just keeps on judging the other one for what he or she is expecting from each other, without thinking that he or she cannot give what he or she does not have. Sometimes the way we show love, is not the way everyone receives love.

Like I said Christians or not, you cannot give what you do not have. Because he or she does not kiss each other when he or she comes home from work does not mean they do not like each other. Who knows why he or she did not get use to that. They might have grown up in a broken home or a broken family or with a single parent. If from growing up what she always saw was her mom fighting her dad for whatever the reasons were, if she chooses to be a sour woman, she will be no matter what. There are men that do not want to go home after work because of those kinds of women. If she wants to be a truly kind woman, she will be a gift for her husband.

But if she grew up with a mother that was strong, lovable, and responsible, she will remember how to do things like her mom, and she will give what she had as memories when she was a child. When a boy always sees his father always mistreating his mom, he will not know how to treat a woman right. If he does not have common sense to say, "I will not act like Dad when I grow up because that is not the right way to treat a woman," the way he saw his dad beat his mother he thought that is the way he is going to act with his wife. Sometimes that boy cannot wait to have a wife to treat that same way, because that is what he can remember.

If he does not ask God to show him how to, he will treat his wife, his mother, or his sister the same way as his dad. They are watching what they see, that is what they will do. Do not judge your spouse ask him or her what is the reason that makes him or her acting that way. A husband that is never give flowers to his wife for her birthday or for Mother's Day, or never takes her out for their anniversary, or he never gives a card or chocolates for Valentine's Day, shows that he does not know how to love but wants to have a family like other people.

DO NOT BE A ROUGH STONE

There is way we should approach someone and ask for something. Nobody likes it when somebody just walks and grabs something that is not theirs. No one should be a rough stone, but us as Christians cannot act like that.

It is true we are adults; that is why sometimes we think as it is okay to talk to other people the way we want or take decisions for people as we please. We always think we can decide for ourselves because we are grown-ups.

What we Christians do not remember is to do not take decisions the way we want for other people because they are our church members or vulnerable. We already know that we must ask God for His will and wait for His answer.

Sometimes, we as believers act like unbelievers too. What we want is what we think that we should get. It is either our way or no way. It cannot be like that because we have a Mighty God that we should put our trust in for anything.

His words are nothing but the truth. Luke 11:9 says, "And I tell you, ask, and it will be given to you; seek, and you will find; knock, and it will be opened to you." We must learn to be patient so we can wait for His will.

We already know if what we have asked God for is not going to be good for us, He will not give it to us. He wants us to always trust in Him because of who He is. A faithful

God.

We do not have to be a rough stone to anyone, because we all are humans we can understand when people are acting right or wrong toward us. We need to learn to put ourselves in other people's shoes too so we can feel how or what they feel.

Even children do not like it when they are playing together to have a rough stone among them. I wonder what makes us think it is okay to act that way with grown up. We are Christians, we should do what is good to other people so the unbelievers can glorify our Lord. We must pay attention to our children, now and after; before losing them by being careless. It does not matter if they call us mean and grouchier parents, but later in life they will thank us; even after we gone. We really need to pay attention to whom they bring home as friends and whom they are playing with, because as parents, that's our responsibility.

WALKING WITH GOD

When we are walking with God, the devil has no power on you. Because your God will work for you. Walking with God means you are a man or a woman of God.

When you are walking with God, you never alone, you are no one's food. When you are walking with God, you are an overcomer. Walking with God makes you feel safer; when you are walking with God, He elevates you.

He makes way when when there seems to be no way. You do not have to worry about anything. No matter what happens it do not have to trouble you; just ask God to give you peace in your mind and in your heart.

He will give it to you because He is peaceful. When you are walking with God, you can be anything by His Grace. And you will love everyone because God is love.

Prayer will be your best friend, if you forget to pray in the morning, you will realize that during the day. You must remember to pray at night, if you fall asleep when you wake up you will have to pray; this is how you will feel.

Walking with God is not a game, it is something profoundly serious. Either you are in it for good, or you are out. If we say we are walking with God, we should have our eyes on God.

We cannot say we are walking with Him, if we have one foot in and one foot out in the world that we left behind or in the world that we were born in. When we take God seriously, He takes us seriously too.

When we walk with God, He will always be the head not the tail. God will always stand for us. He is our fighter; He is our strength and shield. We should always be grateful for His grace and mercy.

When we are taking our responsibilities to walk with God seriously, the devil tries harder to push us to sin more. He brings temptations closer to us, because his plan is to take us to hell with him. James 4:6 says, "Submit yourselves therefore to God. James 4:7 Resist the devil, and he will flee from you."

WALKING WITH GOD THROUGH THE DARK TIME

When we are children of God, we can claim His promises. If we are a child of God, He has a purpose in the darkness for us, because He is preparing us for the bad and the good times.

He wants to show us how faithful He is to us. Do not underestimate what God wants to do in our lives. He loves us so much that is why sometimes He lets us go through trials, storms, and temptations. And when we go there, He always there with us.

He wants us to be strong and faithful to Him. The only thing we must do is trust Him. Remember that He says He will never leave us nor forsake us. So, we know when we have a need where to go. We should know that God wants the best for us.

Upon that basis, we can go to God to answer our prayers. Holiness is a characteristic worthy of spiritual devotion to pray and worship the Almighty God.

Our sins have separated us from the Holy God He came primarily to die on the cross of the calvary so, when there is a need in our lives, we have access to Jesus Christ our Savior.

We need to always remember to pray without cease because the devil is always at work. Do not leave space for him, we do not have room for confusion. When things start to go wrong in our lives, we can understand that is God who wants to make us ready for what is coming for us.

God knows that we must be strong in this life, which is why He wants to be seriously and truthfully committed to our relationship with Him. We must keep the faith. It is true we are not in the world, but we live in this world. We must keep on trusting God to the end of the time in whatever situations we are in.

When Jesus followers agree to follow God, there is not anything that says we are going to be free from trials nor temptations. We know if we are faithfully serving the Almighty with our hearts and souls, we will be at His peace no matter what happens to us.

GREAT RELATIONSHIP WITH GOD

To have a good relationship with God, we must ask Him to give us the strength to be strong in all categories in our lives. We must be humble to always rely on Him, we must be obedient to Him. We must be truthfully committed to Him and only Him. God wants from us to surrender our hearts and souls to Him. To always be in prayers and give Him glory as He created us for. We must live by His will, of course we can think of what we would like to do or accomplish.

But we need to remember if we do not ask Him for what we need and we just do it, if it was not His will, we pay a price for our choice. It is very costly to be foolish.

It is true He gives us free will, where we can choose to serve Him or not to serve Him, but if we choose to serve Him, we must serve Him right. We must learn to take responsibility for our actions. We know we must be faithful to Him. God will never give us a schedule so full that there is no time for Him.

We need to make time in the morning to touch His garments in prayer. We need to be available at midday to continue for the rest of the day, we must count on Him, at night before bedtime, we need to think of Him for a great Father that He is to us. Thank Him for the day, no matter what kind of day it was. We had made it.

We must deeply commit ourselves to the Lord, to have a good relationship with Him. We cannot say we are Christians while we are not concentrating on the words of God: "I have told you these things, so that in me you may have peace. In this world you will have trouble. But take heart! I have overcome the world" (John 16:33). We must have a great relationship with God for this promise to work.

Remember our children are watching us, what we do is what they will do. If they do not see us sincerely with God, they will not be sincere with God. Our children's education is based on the Bible and on the words. A great relationship with God is what every believer should fight for. We know that we do not have to fight the devil because God is fighting him for us, but our relationship with Him is worth every breath that we take because without His breath in our lungs we are nothing.

DEALING WITH TEMPTATION

We must be true believers to be able to deal with temptations. We must have plans to deal with temptations. We should be ready for the devil's attacks on us as we always know that he always at work trying to confuse us.

When an offer comes to us, we need to look for the trap behind that offer. We need to assimilate the Word of God into our lifestyle to form a barrier before the devil's attacks come to us.

Not everything that happens to our lives is God's purpose, but He lets it or lets them happen to change and promote us. It is unscriptural when you are a believer that is not suffering.

To live our lives without Jesus Christ is very foolish because it is very costly for been foolish. We must lean on the Lord Almighty sincerely, and humbly, in prayers. We should make prayer our best friends.

When we are really in pain, it is difficult to concentrate in prayers. Making prayer our best friend will be great for us when we will not be able to concentrate in it. Sometimes we could ask God why He lets us suffer for so long if He loves us.

He lets us suffer for that long for the purpose He has for us. Remember that we never go to pains without God the

Father, no matter storms, temptation, trials, challenges from which we are suffering. He always there, otherwise we would not get out of them by ourselves.

We must keep on going with our faith through Jesus Christ, do not let go because the victory is for the Lord our Savior. God does not want us to fight the devil, He wants us to stand firm in our faith and watch Him work.

POWERFUL PRACTICE OF FASTING

Fasting is about the spirit; if we have a bondage that cannot go away, we can ask God to take that away for us in prayers, because every Christian should be free from bondage.

Fasting is not to persuade God to work faster, but it is to prepare ourselves to listen to God. There are people that always say they can never hear God talking to them.

What they do not know is, if their minds chatter with other things, they will not be able to hear from God. Just because we are not intimate with our spouses or do not eat for two weeks or a month does not mean we are fasting.

Fasting is motivating a desire to hear from God. When we start to fast, everything we place under the rug or in the closet will go to surface because He will clear our minds so we can know the truth, so we can make the right turn.

We are not supposed to be busy for God. So, we can be free from clutter so we can hear and understand what He wants us to do. When we need answers about things, we intend to do we can fast too.

When things are coming our way that we do not understand we can prepare ourselves by fasting so God can show us what is going on or how to be ready to receive what is going to be good for us from the understandable.

Fasting is a devotion to make ourselves available to God. If He says go here or go there so, we can hear Him, and do what He says. To make ourselves available to Him; we must be humble, be good listener and obedient to Him.

Usually, people say when they are going on a diet, that they are fasting as well. Dieting is about the flesh; fasting is not about making us look good. It is about surrender our minds and souls to God.

Fasting is not to show people that we are praying, or to show people that we are Christians, because there are people that are fasting, and they are not even Christians. They are fasting, because they believe if they are going to God with a clean heart and a clear mind, they will hear from the Lord if they are willing to listened.

BENEFITS OF FASTING

We must work on having a greater intimacy with God. This means we will not be able to stay without praying and repentance. We will be always hungry for God's Word.

We will want to have a clean heart so we can pray in peace to be sincerely with God. Genuine fasting results in humility. We must work on our purification so we can have clarity in our minds.

Spiritual discernment is what all Christians need to have in their lives. Sometimes we will be able to understand things in a heartbeat. To be able to have vision of what God wants us to know or see.

Fasting is fruitless if it attempts to impress others. Fasting is fruitless if it is for a religious ritual. Like I said earlier we must devote ourselves to God for us to understand God's love.

When we have a clear mind, it will be easier to ask God for directions for our lives and to enabling power in our lives. For whatever God surfaces in our heart, He will enable us to do.

Fasting should be widespread practice among Jesus Christ's followers. Fasting is not for persuasion, but for preparation to meet with the Lord our God. Fasting is about removing distractions that keep us from focusing on God.

So that your fasting will not be noticed by men, but by your father who is in secret; and your father who sees what is done in secret will reward you.

–Matthew 6:18

And when you fast, do not look gloomy like the hypocrites, for they disfigure their faces that their fasting may be seen by others. Truly, I say to you, they have received their reward.

–Matthew 6:16.

We should know that fasting does not speed up God's will. Fasting will not persuade God to do something that is not His will.

WHY DO NOT WE LISTEN TO GOD?

We often do not listen to God, because we do not believe that persistent ideas we have are God's way of talking to us. Sometimes we are too busy to listen to Him. Or we are too afraid of what God will say to us.

As Jesus followers we need to know how to identify God's voice. God is very consistent with His Word. He speaks quietly and He speaks clearly. God speaks to us through His Word, He speaks through prayer.

He can speak to us through other people or through circumstances. If we do not pay attention to listen to God, He will use difficult and painful situations to get our attention.

God's guidance is of no value unless we are willing to listen. To receive God's guidance requires us to give Him time to speak. After He called the crowd to Him again, He began saying to them, "Listen to Me, all of you, and understand" (Mark 7:14).

> *"If anyone has ears to hear, let him hear." And he said to them, "Pay attention to what you hear..."*
>
> **–Mark 4:23-24.**

God speaks to us because He wants to give us clear directions.

Turn our hearts to God when we are quiet and tell God that we are willing to listen to Him. We will have to listen more carefully. Developing and listening to the heart is particularly important thing. We need to practice making it right with God. Can we count the times in twenty-four hours that we spend listening to God?

We must do our best to be good listeners always so we can hear God's voice, this is especially important in our lives as Christians to hear His voice. I cannot say how grateful I have been when I have had heard God's voice call me by my real name.

By my experience, I know that God speaks to everybody, believers or unbeliever, because when He called me to serve Him, I was an idolatress in the world. I listened to His voice. Today, I am not an idolatress anymore, but I am a child of God.

WAYS TO SHOW ENCOURAGEMENT

When we encourage others, we want to build them up. As Christians, a cheerful outlook and a humble spirit with peaceful awareness of God's presence should describe us. We Christians should be grateful that we have the promise of God's protection.

We will have a bodily resurrection, as Christians we are grateful because we can have an intimate relationship with God. We have God's peace in our lives. And we have the unconditional love of God. We have the moment-by-moment presence of God everywhere we go.

As Christians we should be grateful God chooses us. The Holy Spirit dwells in us. We are eternally secure. We have spiritual gifts. As Christians, we should be thoughtful and generous to others.

Encouragement is showing caring concern, and we can do that because that is what we must do to show people how we can care for them. No matter who they are, believers or not. We can give them a call to ask them how they are doing and ask them if they want us to pray especially.

We can encourage them by writing a letter, or we can pray with them. We can give them our full attention, if it possible we can cry with them, because there are touching stories that can make us cry.

We must be patient to people that need encouragement, give a meaningful gift with a smile, agree with them when it is appropriate. Assisting them in an area in which they are really in need of what can be helpful to them.

An affirming look is great to encourage someone. Pass on helpful information is nice to do, but sometimes we must tell the truth and point them to the applicable scripture because the Bible does not lie.

We can encourage people by forgiving them and trying to listen to them. Often people get discouraged because no one wants to listen to them. We must express love to them, we can also make significant impact in someone's life. Show them love and give them a Godly direction.

WHEN WE ARE REALLY IN NEED OF SOMETHING IMPORTANT

I can say nothing is more important than our spiritual lives. We might need to purchase a house or a car. We might have pain that we will want God to take away for us, because we cannot sleep at night.

We might need to go back to school or find a new job so we can leave the one we already have. There are tons of things we might need. That can take months; I will never finish talking about them.

Whatever it might be that we think we need do not go ahead to do God's work for Him, to get what we want. It will not last, later we will regret it, because we did not ask God if it was His will for us to have this or that.

When we ask Him if it is His will for us, for example, to have the car that we wanted, we must be patient to wait and see what God's answer will be. Our timeline is not God's timeline. We may not have patience, but God does things in His own time, and He is never late.

We will be sorry because we did not ask Him for His will and wait for His answer. When we ask Him for His will, if He knows what we ask Him for is not going to be good for us or to cause us to turn our back on Him or to cause our loss, He will not give it to us.

When did not have God in our lives we could think the way we wanted, how we wanted or do whatever we wanted. Now that we are children of God, we cannot think the way we used to anymore. Everything we intend to do we must ask Him for His will.

We do not want to act like before, we just must leave everything to Him and wait, because we do not want to choose our way and play the fool like before. He always keeps His promise, He will do what He says. He is the way maker, the promise keeper.

Our God does not change, He is a faithful God. He is who He says He is. He will always be watching for us and over us as well because He is a formidable God, He wants us to be faithful to Him too, until the end of time.

TRUSTING IN GOD

As Christians our main thing is to put our trust in God. We need to trust God in everything we have in mind, and with everything that we have materially speaking.

Noah expressed courage.

Noah's call to courage is the same as our call to courage: will we do what God says regardless of what He asks? Noah experienced a collision with his society.

When Shadrack, Meshach, and Abednego were in the fire they did not look at the fire, but they looked at God. Because of their trust in God, they had come out alive.

Noah's confrontation is the same as our confrontation: will we obey God when society collides with us? Noah faced a challenge of his faith. Noah's challenge is the same as our challenge: will we do what God says even we do not understand?

> *The Lord saw that the wickedness of man was great in the earth, and that every intention of the thoughts of his heart was only evil continually. And the Lord regretted that he had made man on the earth, and it grieved him to his heart. So the Lord said, "I will blot out man whom I have created from the face of the land, man and animals and creeping things*

and birds of the heavens, for I am sorry that I have made them." But Noah found favor in the eyes of the Lord.

–Genesis 6:5-8

We need to do our best to find favor in the eyes of God. We must ask Him to give us strength so we can be as courageous as Noah. We must obey God in all things. If we do not trust God; who are we going to trust? Who else can direct our ways like Him? We can pray all we want, but if we do not trust God, we are wasting our time.

Trust in the Lord with all your heart and lean not on your own understanding. In all your ways acknowledge Him, and He will make your paths straight. Do not be wise in your own eyes; fear the lord and turn away from evil.

–Proverbs 3:5-6

We must be fully reliant on God because He is trustworthy. We must trust and obey God and leave all the consequences to Him. His will is for us to impact others. Remember that trust in friends might lead to disappointment, but trusting God will take us to the right path and bless us by doing so. We should not doubt God. We must trust that our God will never stop loving us, even in our death bed He will always love us. His love cannot compare to anyone else.

WHAT IS GOD'S PURPOSE?

God's purpose is to introduce His life to our lives. We should be grateful for that. Usually, people think about intimacy as sex or touch or feel. Just being safe is not enough, just going to church is not enough.

Most important thing in our life is having a great relationship with God. Genuine intimacy looks like the ultimate purpose of God created us. To have an intimate relationship with Him, that is what God wants.

If we cannot trust someone, we cannot have an intimate relationship with him or her. We must put our trust in God to say we have a great relationship with Him. As Jesus followers, we already know the main thing God is looking from us is to trust Him.

Because by putting our trust in Him, we already ask Him to help us to be faithful. Even we will have to ask Him to give us the strength to keep on been faithful until the end, He knows what we need, but He wants us to open our mouths to ask for the things that we need.

The same way He knows what we did wrong, but He wants us to open our mouths to tell Him what we did wrong when we ask for forgiveness. God does not want us to say, "Father, you know I am wrong." He wants us to be honest with Him.

There is an enormous difference between loving God or having affection for God. We can have an intimate relationship with God, but if we do not have patience to wait for God to answer our prayers! We are wasting our time.

When we say we do not have time to pray, this means we do not have time for God, because when we finish to pray, we must wait to listen to God. That is why most relationships do not work, because one person does all the talking and do not willing to listen.

We must have time for the Lord, we should meditate on His words, we should always find time to talk to God, no matter how things are going in our lives, we should not give up on Him. God does not pay for pleasure, but He pays for being available to do what He wants us to do.

WHAT DOES GOD WANT?

God wants us to seek His way. God created us to follow Him sincerely, He wants to make us Godly. When we ask God to show us His will, we should not leave God's path. We must bid with Him, to have the courage to wait for His answer.

We must honor God with our wealth, not only money but with our time, our talent, our heart, and strength. We want His favor on us and on our families. We must be obedient to the Almighty God.

Oftentimes we are looking for answer everywhere like crazy, but we never think of looking for the answers in the Bible, in the Word of God. There are times we preferred to ask families and friends for their opinions than to ask God what He thinks about what is going on in our lives.

If we can trust our business partners, our friends, our families, or a therapist when we have plans to do something, why not put our trust in God? He wants us to depend on Him, and on nobody else. No one can think better than God for us. There is no other way to please the Lord, but trust Him, listen to Him, and be obedient to Him.

He knows that we are not perfect, but if we ask Him to help us, we can try our best to do what He wants us to do. Because we must try to do better more than ever to arrange ourselves with God.

The world is changing in front of us, things are getting out hand, there is pushing and shoving everywhere. Things are getting harder every day, only God knows what is going on. We must be ready for whatever will come our way. That is why we call ourselves Christians.

As Christ followers we should always depend on Jesus Christ by trusting Him and faithful to Him. Like Jesus Christ always praying His Father, before He does anything, we should do the same. And we must always continue to serve God faithfully so, we must have a strong life by obey the whole truth of the Word of God so we can do our best to walk saved.

FILLED WITH THE HOLY SPIRIT

When we are filled with the Holy Spirit, we are living under His prevailing control that requires surrender. Which means we repented of our all-known sin. When we ask, we must believe that we will receive what we have asked for.

Our failures help us recognize that the Holy Spirit came to enable us to live godly lives that we cannot live apart from Him. The Holy Spirit enables believers to do God's work and to live a Godly life.

Baptism of the Holy Spirit is the work of God at salvation that places us into Christ and makes us part of His body. As we can see as soon as we repent and baptize, our salvation is starting right there. This means we must take our spiritual lives seriously.

We are qualified to preach the Word, which means the gospel of Jesus Christ. That He calls us to do. If we are keeping our word with God, we can ask Him to help us to be faithful and humble, so, we can always in prayer. He will send the Holy Spirit to give us the strengths to get the job done.

"And Peter said to them, 'Repent and be baptized every one of you in the name of Jesus Christ for the forgiveness of your sins, and you will receive the gift of the Holy Spirit'" (Act 2:38).

And I will ask the Father, and he will give you another Helper, to be with you forever, even the Spirit of truth, whom the world cannot receive, because it neither sees him nor knows him. You know him, for he dwells with you and will be in you.

–John 14:15-17

But when the Helper comes, whom I will send to you from the Father, the Spirit of the truth who proceeds from the Father. He will bear witness about me. And you also bear witness because you have been with me from the beginning.

–John 15:26-27

GUIDED BY THE HOLY SPIRIT

Jesus' mission is to introduce us to the power of the Holy Spirit. To teach us how to love and to forgive others, to teach us how to pray. His mission is also to reveal the Father to redeem the fallen humankind and revive the hope of those looking for the Messiah.

Jesus sent the Holy Spirit to dwell in us that we cannot be a part of Him and to keep us stronger, otherwise we will not be able to do what Jesus Christ calls us to do. The Holy Spirit will show us what to do, which decision to make, how to follow Christ, and how to be Christ-like.

He will guide us in the right path. Which is the right path of Jesus Christ our Savior and Lord. We should be always wise in Jesus Christ's name, because a wise person will listen to the Holy Spirit. We need to learn to spend time with God alone in prayer. This is the connection we must have with God.

We cannot find ourselves too busy for God. The whole connection in our lives is our relationship with the Almighty God. He is the One we go to for everything. He is the One we ask for everything. He should be the One we ask if it is His will for everything we need or will want in life.

Strong is our connection with God the Father, God the Son, and God the Holy Spirit. We must show our children how to have a great relationship with God. So, they know when and how to respond to trials, tribulations, temptations, storms, challenges and all the rest.

If we do not show them how to pray, how to trust God as their Heavenly Father that they must go to always for anything in life such as joy, pains, happiness, sorrows. Teach them how to spends times in prayer with God. Teach them also the Almighty God is their God too. To always try to listen to God by learning to hear God's voice, learn to obey God and not worry about the consequences. God will take care of the consequences.

GUIDED BY THE HOLY SPIRIT

We as parents we have the responsibilities to remind our children to pray the Almighty God every day! We must show our children how to pray otherwise we are going to hurt them and deny them, because they will find out they will have to learn about God themselves.

They need to know who God is, they need to know what prayer is; they must know they have to be available for God in their lives. There is not even one of us who does not have time to pray to Him. If we tell God that we are too busy to pray, He will bring challenges to us so we can find time to pray to Him.

Train up a child in the way he should go; even when he is old, he will not depart from it.

–Proverbs 22:6

God is a daily discipline in our lives, God is first in our lives. God is who we should start our day with always. And the second is our relationship with Him. Our strong life stays upon the teaching of the word of God and their applications of them.

We must remember the sound of the Word of God, because it is an extremely sweet and important sound in for our lives.

I know God is the One that order our steps, but there are

times we try to do what we want without asking God if it is His will. The time is now to start arranging our lives with Him, because we already know what we must do to live a Godly life. Because in God's eyes we are all holy.

We need to always remember that our time is not ours; we belong to God. He creates us to do good works and serving and giving glory to Him. It is true we can have fun, but we must watch what kind of conversations that we take part in or are about to take part in, because the Holy Spirit will not take part in corrupt or vain conversations.

I know that we are not supposed to judge, but we really need to be careful of who we are talking to; there are times we do not expect the kind of language, just stop right there. If asked why we stopped, we can answer that we are not comfortable with these kinds of conversations anymore or we do not speak this kind of language anymore. Yes, I used to talk that way, but not anymore. Now that I have become a new person, I must watch what I am saying, because I do not want to push away the Holy Spirit. WHO IS WORTHY?

GUIDED BY THE HOLY SPIRIT

Everybody is worthy in the eyes of God because Jesus Christ died for all humans being. Jesus of Nazareth preached the gospel to all humankind. We must do the same, we cannot choose those to whom to preach the gospel. We can do everything under the sun in church, if we do not do the job that Jesus Christ calls us to do, we are wasting our time.

> *And Jesus came and said to them, "All authority in heaven and on earth has been given to me. Go therefore and make disciples of all nations, baptizing them in the name of the Father and of the Son and of the Holy Spirit, teaching them to observe all that I have commanded you. And behold, I am with you always, to the end of the age."*
>
> **–Matthew 28:18-20**

No matter how we preach the gospel, we must do it if we answer the call that Jesus Christ trusts us with! There are people that are dying because they do not know about our Jesus Christ. We do not need to know someone to tell him or her that Jesus of Nazareth is coming. We need to be proud of the gospel of God or of the Word of God. We all need to remember our values do not come from what we have, or what kind of car we are driving. Our values come from Jesus Christ our Lord and Savior.

We must be wise to preach the gospel, but do not think we can be wisely doing it without the Holy Spirit help. Without Him, we will be too tired to go, we will be too sick to go, we will be too lazy to go, we will be too busy to go. We must be smart to recognize the devil's games.

When you give them a flyer or a pamphlet that stated the message that we have talked to them about, *Jesus is coming soon*, with the Bible references where it says Jesus Christ is coming soon, this will make more sense to them.

That is all we must do, our job is to give the message, as we are supposed to do so. Let the Holy Spirit do His part. We cannot do anything for anyone who had not accepted Christ, but I've seen what He did in my life! And in our lives, they can come to Christ if they choose to. Now days we can use the social media groups to preach the gospel. For example: Matthew 3:2 says, "Repent, for the kingdom of heaven is at hand."

THE HOLY SPIRIT: AN ABSOLUTE ESSENTIAL

God is very truthful that there is no one like Him, that is why He is who He is. He cannot lie. That is why He does not like liars, which is also why He does not want us to lie about anything. God wants us to be real and serious to follow Him and Him alone.

Our God is unchanging, He will be always the same. That is why we must pour out our hearts before Him; in all our ways acknowledge Him, because His faithfulness will never end. God is Omniscient. He knows all things, we cannot hide anything from Him, because He is light, He can see everything that in the dark, in the closets or under the rugs.

God is Omnipotent. He has all power. That is why He gives us power over the devil, He gives the power to pray for people in need, to pray for sick people and He gives us power to take authority over the devil. And He says if we believe in Him, we will do more than He did when He was living among us.

> *Truly, truly, I say to you, whoever believes in me will also do the work that I do; and greater work than these will he do, because I am going to the Father.*
>
> **–John 14:12.**

Our God is Omnipresent, all things are in His presence. No matter where we are, God knows. Our families might not know, our friends, or our church members might not know, but the presence of God will always be everywhere, because He has the world in His hand.

God stays behind every word He says. When we think God is silent that is when He is fulfilling our promises; when we think we are still sick, we do not even realize that God already cured us. We as Christians need to learn from God to be real with ourselves.

We do not need to lie to get a job or a position, to get a woman or a man to love us. We do not need to change ourselves to fit in any group or anywhere. We are supposed to show the real us because we will never be good enough for anybody. God is the one who knows us more than anyone! We must change our ways, our minds, and lifestyles so we can have a great relationship with Him. That is all we need.

THE CHARACTERISTICS OF GOD

There are people that can be in church years after years and they never grow because they never encounter the Holy Spirit. The Holy Spirit is somebody you are not praying to get. The Holy Spirit is somebody you are looking to get.

The Holy Spirit is not a power. The Holy Spirit comes to enable us to do the work God calls us to do. It is very importance to ask God what it is He wants us to do. Often people have difficulty living the Christian life, because they want to live the Christian life with their own strength and their pride.

We cannot say we want to be filled with the Holy Spirit and not want to go down the right path. Jesus Christ sent the Holy Spirit to direct our paths. If we are not believers, we will do it alone. He says He will carry our burdens.

When we surrender our lives to Him, the Holy Spirit will seal us. And the Holy Spirit is someone that we will receive at the baptism day. This is how our lives are, hidden in Christ as the Bible says.

Sometimes we need to stop been hardheaded so we can listen to the Holy Spirit's voice, because if He can guide us, that means we can hear Him talking to us too. It is extremely easy for the devil to find place in our minds, and in our hearts, if we let him too. By the power of the blood of Jesus Christ and the strength of the Holy Ghost, we can push him far away from us.

When the Holy Spirit Show us how to behave, sometimes we might think we can go overboard when we are having conversations at work, with our friends and families. Right away we will have a common sense that tells us do not to do this or that or stop what we are doing or about to do. That is the Holy Spirit helping us go on the right path.

As Christians there is no way, we can live without the Holy Spirit. Otherwise, we will be like a car without brakes and lights on the dark peach road at night. Like I said before, there are people that are going to church for years and those that were born in the Christian families that never encounter the Holy Spirit in their lives. We must take a step closer to Christ every single day in our lives, and we will be glad we did. If not, spiritually, we will not grow.

GOD'S MERCY

The mercy of God never ceases, but if we chose to refuse God, reject Him, or act rebellious against Him or like we do not need Him, He can allow us to die without repentance. We cannot explain God's mercy, but we can explain His love. We are where we are because of the grace of God, because of His mercy. We would be foolish to deny the grace and the mercy of God.

God's mercy and His compassion renew every day, every morning before we even waking up. His grace will never end. His compassion will never change. Which means our God will never change. That is why we must serve Him faithfully; we need to take our relationship with the Almighty God seriously because when we expect punishment for what we do wrong, instead of that we found mercy from Him. We must take our Spiritual lives serious. And we must do that right now!

And the time to change is right now! Anyone can change if they want to. We do not have time to play around with our spiritual lives anymore. We need to be available to read the Bible, this is our meditation. The Bible is what that can help us keep on going. They can try to make us feel good in church, but we should know better. Without concentration in the Word of God, we will not be able to cope with whatever that will come to us or throwing at us.

Yes! We have the Holy Spirit when we were born again by the grace of God, but we must watch carefully how our relationship is with God because we cannot start serving the Lord and choose to stop whenever we want. It does not work that way. We know the enemy is always at work so we can fall at any time that he finds a chance.

Do not leave space for the devil to make us fall, block him here and there so we can be victorious with the strength and the blood of Jesus Christ our Savior. We need to remember, it does not matter if we have diplomas and certificates, or money or gold, we will not be able to serve the Lord by ourselves without the Holy Spirit's help.

If we ever think that way, we will fall, we will look back and the devil will win in his games. And another thing we need to always put in mind that we do not go to church to be place holder for no one, nor to go warm up the benches or chairs for nobody. Jesus said unto him, "No one who puts his hand to the plow and looks back is fit for the kingdom of God" (Luke 9:62).

PAY ATTENTION WHEN PRAYING WITH PEOPLE OVER THE PHONE

After talking to one of my church members, she told me what happened to her. I told her, "If it was me, I would ask God for forgiveness and never do that again."

She asked me, "Will I be okay to do a twenty-one-days prayer with you?"

I said, "Yes, I will do it with you, let me look at my calendar, then I let you know when we can start."

Every day after work, I put my bag away and started the prayer with her just like that. I did not want to do anything before I started the prayer with her, because I did not want to get discouraged if I had to wait after taking a shower and having supper before I could help her.

To me, it was better to start the prayer as soon as I made it home, then I could relax later in the afternoon. One night I went to sleep, I had a dream, I saw there were people from my church that were about to go away, and I said, "Wait for me, I am going with you."

When I looked at my clothes, they were dirty. I said, "Give me ten minutes to change my clothes so I can go with you."

When I went inside to change my clothes that is when I realized that my clothes were clean. I went back outside so I could go with them, but the car had already left.

Usually I would go on my knees to thank God for the great night that I had, but that morning after I thanked Him, I said, "Lord, I do not understand what is going on; but you know everything, please help me find out what is going on, because my clothes should not be dirty on me."

I said, "I know nobody is perfect but You the Father, Jesus the Son, and the Holy Spirit. I am not fornicating, killing, hurting my neighbors, I do not steal, I do not make anybody lose his or her job, I do not involve myself in idols anymore, I do not look back, I do not ask you to let me know what I did wrong that could make me feel dirty, because I am neither clean nor holy, but I ask you all these in the name of Your Son Jesus Christ. I pray, amen."

After pleading on my knees before the Almighty God that morning, I have kept on asking God to help me find out what was wrong.

PAY ATTENTION WHEN PRAYING WITH PEOPLE OVER THE PHONE

I did not stop until God helped me realize what was happening while I was praying with her. Five days later I heard someone talking to her, while we were praying.

That person asked her who she was. She answered, "That is my church member, we are doing a twenty-one-day together." I heard him say, "You are not supposed to pray with people, you should pray by yourself."

For that reason, I agreed to pray with her! That was the same thing she was still doing. God showed me my clothes were dirty because He wanted to show me that the problem was still there, to not waste my time. We can choose to help sometimes, without knowing what we are putting ourselves in to. It may be things that can affect our spiritual lives. Do not forget to ask God if we allowed to do so.

I had to do twenty-one-day by myself to ask God for forgiveness, because I was praying with someone in church and still dealing with sorcery and idols.

We need to ask God before we agree to pray with people. That does not mean if we were talking on the phone with our church members, we cannot pray with them before we hang up.

There is an enormous difference between praying with someone we were talking on the phone with and praying over the phone with somebody for forgiveness or for something special, either for three-day, for seven-day, for twenty-one day, or forty-day plans. After what happened to me, I ask God please to make me remember to ask Him before I take charge praying with anyone.

I will still go pray with people in the hospitals, in nursing homes, or house prayers, but over the phone never again without God's permission other than my kids. There are things we do not know about our church members, but God the Almighty knows. Like I said, I had to pray and ask God for forgiveness, because I did not ask Him if I could pray with her.

To be honest, I did not know that I needed to ask God if I could pray with anyone. I was taught praying with someone was okay to do; so, I did.

There are consequences when we do not ask God if that person is someone that we can be a prayer partner with.

DIED IN OURSELVES

There is no limit for people who died in themselves. If we die in ourselves, we will be able to follow the words of God. We will be able to hear the Holy Spirit voice to guide us on the right path. We need to know that we are nothing more than a corn seed that needs to die so we can germ to become a new corn plant.

"Died in ourselves" means to let go of everything we used to do. Let go of the pride that we put in our minds. We need to stop on doing whatever we want whenever we want without asking God what His plan for our lives is; we need to wait for His answer. We cannot keep on pleasing people to make them feel good, or to make them like us, then telling them the truth.

God wants us to put Him first, in everything, He wants to be our friend too, not only our Father. God's plan is different from ours; His thinking is also different from ours: "For I know the plans I have for you, declares the Lord, plans for welfare and not for evil, to give you a future and a hope" (Jeremiah 29:11).

When died in ourselves, because we know Jesus Christ as our Personal Savior, this molds our character, impacts our beliefs, influences our lifestyles, and determines our eternal destiny.

God as the Potter molds our character to change us the way He wants us to be. That is why we need to take pride off our minds, with it we will not change, we will not give all the glory to God. We will not continue to be humble if we keep pride in our minds. We need to let go of everything; we cannot let go of them halfway.

The Christian's life is not easy, but if we really concentrate on serving the Lord with sincerity, we will see how easy the Lord is going to make it for us. Because the way we serve the Lord, that is what that will be counted.

So, to die in ourselves will be the best thing that will happens to us. We will feel confident in the Lord Jesus Christ. No matter how big a challenge can be or will be! We will be able to stand in front of it, with the blood of the Holy Lamb of God. There is nothing else we can do better to serve the Lord than die in ourselves. Dying in ourselves is what every Jesus Christ follower must do.

HOW GOD GETS OUR ATTENTION

God gets our attention by not answering our prayers, and He gets our attention by letting us do what we please. When we realize that things did not go as planned, that is when we start asking God questions. *What happens to us? Why does He hear and let all these things happen to us?*

If we are not obedient and humble to Him, we will have the feeling of doing what we want, whenever we want. That is when God tries to get our attention. God loves us; He does not want to punish us for what we do wrong, but He knows how to makes us give Him the attention that He deserves.

There are people that become ill, or lose their jobs, or lose things that are important to them. That is when they start to look at God, and they start to pray. We are all humans, but there are Christians that like to learn the hard way. Our Father God is very patient, no one has His patience.

He always gives us time to repent, time to bring our attentions to Him. Often, we give our attention to family and friends or our co-workers than giving attention to God. And God is supposed to be the first One to get our attentions. We must remember to pay attention to the Almighty because He is the Alpha and Omega. He is the biggening and the end.

We should not wait for God to look for attention from us,

we must always be on our knees, we must always give Him the glory that He deserves. And we should take time to think about every single morning we wake up without an oxygen tank or a breathing tube. Thanking God every morning for waking us up will show Him how grateful that we are to Him.

That right there is giving Him attention. When we set up our alarms to wake us up on time. That feels great right, but can that alarm wake the ones that are in deep sleep too? God's grace renews every morning for everybody on the earth that is still breathing, as Jesus Christ followers we are not supposed to be ungrateful to God our Father. Remember that if we do not give God the attention He deserves He will look for it from us.

TITHES AND OFFERINGS

Paying or giving tithes and offerings is an act of obedient to the Almighty God. He asks us to give 10% of our revenues, or of what we are taking home when we get paid. Ten percent, that is all He is asking for as the tithes.

As for the offerings, that is up to us, we can give what we can, but the tenth percent is obligatory. We cannot ever repay God for what He has done for us. By being grateful to Him, we can give a reasonable amount for offerings.

There are people that say tithes were for the time of when the Levitz were serving at the Sanctuary. If tithes and offerings were for when the Levitz were taking care of the Sanctuary, why do we say the Bible is there for our instructions?

These things were there before the first coming of Jesus of Nazareth, and after He went to heaven sitting at the right of His Father. We must read the Word of God to help us understand better when we say the Bible is there for our instructions, that we do not think the Bible is there for what we want or like to do only. The Bible is there for every instruction without exceptions whatsoever.

We must pray God to help us understand how to be good listeners, so we can be obedient to Him now to the end of time. Jesus followers or believers are saying God is unchangeable, He is the same before, yesterday, today, and forever. Yet why, when it comes to tithes and offerings? It was the time of the Levitz service in the Solomon temple.

Malachi 3:10 says, "Bring the full tithe into the storehouse, that there may be food in my house. And thereby put me to the test, says the Lord of hosts, if I will not open the windows of heaven for you and pour down for you a blessing until there is no more need."

We need to remember that we were born selfish. I am sure you know that babies do not care when they are wet, hungry, or uncomfortable, and they will let you know. We are generously born again. We were born greedy; we are born again a giver. The way God does not make a minor change in us, that is how we need to stop giving the left-over change in our purses for offerings, because God did not say how much we should give.

TITHES AND OFFERINGS

For it will be like a man going on a journey, who called his servants and entrusted to them his property. To one he gave five talents, to another two, to another one, to each according to his ability. Then he went away. He who had received the five talents went at once and traded with them, and he made five talents more. So also he who had the two talents made two talents more. But he who had received the one talent went and dug in the ground and hid his master's money. Now after a long time the master of those servants came and settled accounts with them. And he who had received the five talents came forward, bringing five talents more, saying, "Master, you delivered to me five talents; here, I have made five talents more." His master said to him, "Well done, good and faithful servant. You have been faithful over a little; I will set you over much. Enter into the joy of your master." And he also who had the two talents came forward, saying, "Master, you delivered to me two talents; here, I have made two talents more." His master said to him, "Well done, good and faithful servant. You have been faithful over a little; I will set you over much. Enter into the joy of your master." He also who had received the one talent came forward, saying, "Master, I knew you to be a hard man, reaping where you did not sow, and gathering where you scattered no seed, so I was afraid, and I went and hid your talent in the ground. Here, you have what is yours." But his master answered him, "You wicked and slothful servant! You knew that I reap where I have not sown and gather where I scattered no seed? Then you ought to have invested my money with the bankers, and at my coming I should have received what was my own with interest. So take the talent from him and give it to him who has the ten talents. For to everyone who has will more be given, and he will have an abundance. But from the one who has not, even what he has will be taken away. And cast the worthless servant into the outer darkness. In that place there will be weeping and gnashing of teeth."

–Matthew 25:14-30

We are watching God's things; they are not ours. By paying tithes and offerings, we will bless more every day.

TITHES AND OFFERINGS

Very often spouses that do not have a good relationship have tough times sharing a bank account together. When it comes to paying tithes and offerings, if one of them is willing to pay tithes and offerings, the other one might say, "I do not need to pay tithes and offerings because my wife or my husband and I are one. Since he or she pays tithes and offerings, I do not have to."

It is true when you are married you are becoming one flesh, but God will see and understand if one of you does not have a job. When both of you are working, you should add together what you are getting paid and subtract the ten percent of what you are bringing home to pay the tithes and offerings.

As for the offerings, it depends on you to choose a reasonable amount to give for that. If you and your spouse choose to take the ten percent before taxes, which means from your gross pay, or if you want to take it from your net pay. If the ten percent comes from your gross pay, you will not have to give the ten percent from your tax return.

If we remember to pay tithes and offerings the way God asking us to do, we will be great by showing Him that we are obedient to Him. The same way we must be faithful to the Almighty God, the way we must preach the gospel all over the world. That is the same way we must always pay tithes and offerings. Tithes and offerings are an act of obedience to God. Remember that we can always give without love, but we cannot love without give. Those who are kind benefit themselves but the cruel bring ruin on themselves.

ASKING, SEARCHING, AND KNOCKING

When we are asking the Lord for anything, we must believe and think we already have it, says our Lord and Savior. Mark 11:24 says, "Therefore I tell you, whatever you ask in prayer, believe that you have received it, and it will be yours."

When we ask for something, we must have patience to wait for God to give it to us. We need to remember if what we are asking God for is something that is going to be good for us. Of course He will give it to us, but if it is something that is going to cause our loss, God will not give it to us.

After a year or two years of asking for something, if we do not receive it, we must know that's not what God want to give to us, we are not ready to receive what we are asking for, or that is not God's will for us.

We must search to have a great relationship with God primarily: "Seek first the kingdom of God, and His righteousness, and all these things shall be added to you" (Matthew 6:33).

We can search for whatever we think that can be good for us or to fulfill our needs. If we do not search for God's presence every day in our lives, we are wasting our time.

God is our Creator. He is the one that created man, He said it was good, but He realized it was not okay for man to be alone. That is why He created a woman to be with the man that He created. That can show us, God did not create us to be alone without a partner by marriage.

We, as Jesus' followers, do not need to search for someone to get married to. God knows what we need, that does not mean we do not have to ask Him for what we need. We just must put our trust Him. Even though we think we know what we want, and what we are searching for, we have no idea if we do not ask God if it is His choice to let us know or if it is not His choice to let us know.

If we think we can choose whomever we please because we are getting older, we will be sorry, because the outcome will not be good. That is when we will regret that we did not ask God if it was His will for us.

ASKING, SEARCHING, AND KNOCKING

When searching everywhere like crazy without asking God, we will pay the price for that. And when we are asking God if that is the man or the woman that He wants for us, we must wait for God's answer. Because our thinking is not God's thinking, and God does things in His own time. He will not rush like us, and He is never late, He is always on time.

We must wait for God's choice, we must trust Him and not just go ahead and do what we want because we could not wait. When things starting to go wrong with our choices that is when we realize if we go to Him to ask for forgiveness maybe He will fix things for us. I know He is a forgiving Father, but only He can decide if it will be too late for us to ask for forgiveness or not.

We do not need to search for anything other than His kingdom as He says and to have a great relationship with Him. Remember that He is the creator of everything, He can give or bless us with anything that will be good for us.

Matthew 7:7-8 says, "Ask, and you will receive, search, and you will find. Knock and the door will be open to you." For everyone who asks will receive, for everyone who searches will find, for everyone who knocks the door will be opened.

We must knock on God's door always, to seek His presence because He wants our attention. Knock on His door in the morning, in the evening, and before we go to bed at night. Knocking on God's door will keep our relationship stronger with Him. And that is going to make God open His door to forgive us when we feel like we need to go to Him to ask for repentance.

Another thing we should know and remember if we are not opening the doors of our hearts to God and His Son and the Holy Spirit to enter! We will be wasting our time knocking on His door. I know He is who He says He is. He will provide and do what He has promised us. We just need to open our hearts to serve Him the way He wants us to. And we will live a happier life with joy and peace in our hearts.

No one cannot tell us to stop asking God for what we need, but what we need to ask God is to fight the devil for us so we can stay under His wings until the day we die. Because the devil's game is for us to not see what he left forever in heaven.

WE MUST KNOW WHO WE ARE

As Jesus' followers we must be incredibly careful about who we are. We need to pay attention to our manners. It is extremely easy to see what is going on in other people's lives than to see what is going on in our lives and take responsibilities of our problems. We already know it will not be easy to change the bad attitude and habits that we have.

Only thing to do is to pray harder by asking the Almighty God to help us change those bad habits so we can serve Him better. Anything we want to change or any mess we think that must be removed from our lives, that we cannot get rid of just take them to God now! We must ask God to give us the strength to stay in prayer, to be humble to Him always, to hide us under His garments. So, the Holy Spirit can be with us to guide us from any bad ideas. Because there will be bad ideas.

We need to seek God's presence without ceasing so He can watch over our spiritual lives. We must keep our eyes on the Lord and the Lord only. Our spiritual life is extremely important! We cannot call ourselves Christians or believers without the Holy Spirit in our lives. It will look like we washed our hands and put them back in the dust again. When we say yes, we should mean it, and when we say no, we must mean no.

Believers! We do not have to prove nothing to anyone, but to prove God by the blood of His holy Son that we can be sincere and faithful to Him, we must be sincere to everyone. If cannot be sincere to people we can see, people to whom we can talk, how can we be sincere to God that we cannot see and feel?

Other people's pain should be ours because Jesus' followers must be Christlike. We will not be able to take away their pain, but we can help them pray, so Jesus Christ can take away their pain. It is especially important to pay attention to what we are doing while we are living in this world. Because the devil is real and playing every game that he can think of; the devil is everywhere, and so are his agents.

His agents are there to make people do what they are not supposed to do, but if we continue to keep our eyes open on Jesus of Nazareth our Lord and Savior, He will defeat the devil for us so we can stay and be spiritual for the rest of our lives.

WE MUST KNOW WHO WE ARE

It is a great thing when you are somewhere, and you have heard someone say, "That if it was not for you as a Christian that was here, I would tell him or her." I did not ask her what she wanted to say, but I got a feeling whatever she wanted to say to that person was not going to sound good. I was happy she thought that way towards Christians. If an unbeliever has respect for us as Christians, don't you think we must respect ourselves to not do what Christians are not supposed to do nor be involved in?

Watch ourselves and our children that are what we must do best. People are looking at us and at our kids because we are Christians. Believers or not they are watching what we are doing. They may not say anything to us to let us know, but they are observing us. Once we are born again, we already say bye to the world. Anything that can mess up our spiritual lives must be buried now. We do not need to plant them but destroy them.

There are things we cannot wear anymore, there are things that we cannot do anymore. Do not say that we need to work on those things, it will not be easy to work on those things by yourself because the devil is a liar, but by God in Jesus Christ He can make changes in your life if you let Him.

Same here if we want to work on our spiritual lives. Go to

God by His Son Jesus Christ, He will make it happen. If we feel like we must work hard to achieve our dreams, work well and pray harder because anything is possible with Jesus Christ. Whatever we must do, do it now! Because tomorrow is not promised. Right now is the time to do what we think that we must do. Today is the day to start working on whatever goals on which we must work.

They say whoever you spend time together with, that is who you are. There are a couple co-workers that I used to go to lunch with. Another co-worker asked them if I was a smoker too, but they never let me know about that. One day we were on our way to lunch, the one that has asked him the question about me was walking out to lunch too. The one the question was asked to said, "You know what, this guy asked me if you smoke too. I told him no you do not smoke, and you are a Christian." Then I said in my mind, *I must stop going to lunch with them.* I realized I started to gain weight by eating junk food, so I stopped going to lunch with them.

CAUGHT UP IN A BAD SITUATION AS BELIEVERS

There was a downpour night. A neighbor had a charcoal grill that she used to cook food for her family, and it was soaked that night. Those charcoal grills can have three to four foyers. She did not have a kitchen inside the house, nor an outside space to build one. In the island countries, not everyone can afford a stove or to have a kitchen inside their homes. Sometimes they can find a little space outside, and they can cover the top of that little space to cook as their kitchen.

In the morning when she got out to go to her business, she moved that charcoal grill to the sunny position so it could dry. One Christian neighbor stole it. When that lady came back home, she was looking for that charcoal grill, but she could not find it. She knocked on every neighbors' door that lived close to her and asked them if they did not see a charcoal grill outside for her. They said no, they did not see it, even the Christian that stole it.

That day, the charcoal grill owner could not cook for her family because of that. The neighbor that took the charcoal grill forgot if he should not do that kind of thing or if it was a habit for him, who knows? We are not here to judge anyone, only God knows if it was a mistake or a habit.

One night he had a dream, in that dream he saw Jesus Christ's second coming. He was incredibly happy to go meet Him in the clouds. He saw there was a rapture, and he was one of those who started to go up in the air to go meet the Lord. He said that he and the others started singing a song that he had never heard before. He saw they were going up together, they kept on singing while they passed the clouds. No one was higher than another one, but he started to see the other believers' feet going up in the air, he thought they were faster than him, and how could that be? He wondered what was going on because they were at the same height. He realized that he was the one that started going down.

When he looked down, he saw the charcoal grill was tied on his waist. Charcoal grills were made with iron, and he became heavier by having that thing tied to his waist. That was why he could not continue to go further with the others, to go meet the Lord as every Christian plans to do.

CAUGHT UP IN A BAD SITUATION AS BELIEVERS

In the morning when he woke up, he waited for when there was no one outside in that neighborhood watching. He took the charcoal grill back to where he had found it. That was a wake-up call for him, he learned the hard way to not steal other peoples' belongings.

God is really a great God!

Look how God made him realized if he did not leave that thing where he had found it, he would not go anywhere.

God is a Father with love, and grace and compassion.

The way He showed him that thing could have stopped him from going to heaven, that was his story. He let go of what was not his after he found out what would happen to him if he did not change his behavior.

Every one of us as Jesus Christ followers have a story that can stop us from going to heaven. Because I do not know what can stop you to go to heaven, or you do not know what can stop me from going to heaven, does not mean that God does not know what we are hiding or whatever habits that can stop us to have eternal life. We all know what must change in us all, to be able to go to our destination that is heaven. That is every Christian's dream, going to live with the Lord our God.

Each one of us as believers knows if we have things that can stop us from going to heaven. Our church members, our pastors, our friends, and family members may not know, but remember there is someone that is always there because He is omnipresent, He knows what sin we are petting, and what kind sin with which we are playing. The best thing we must do is to take them to the Lord because all is possible with Him. Whatever it is that can cause us to be lost must change now! Because we have a hell to watch out for and a heaven to gain.

Because it is not worth saying we are something that the Almighty God knows that we are not. We cannot waste our time going to church if do not have a good relationship with God. We will be foolish to be active in church and later lose our souls. I said that already, and I am saying it again, we must open our hearts and souls to serve the Lord sincerely and faithfully with our both feet, both our eyes, and both hands in the church.

Not one foot, one hand, and eye in the church, and one out in the world. We must have a clear conscience and a heart fully surrendered to Jesus Christ. We need to pay attention to God's voice, so we can stop whatever we are doing to listen to God.

CAUGHT UP IN A BAD SITUATION AS BELIEVERS

When He wants to speak to us, always look for His presence and give Him glory. He wants us to be faithful to Him, obedient to Him, to be humble to Him, to not have any other god before Him, to fully surrender our hearts and souls to Him so we can have a great relationship with Him. If we open our hearts and souls to serve Him, there is no way we will not make it to heaven because that is the plan.

Our God is the greatest, He is the God above all gods. His name is above all names. There is nothing that is strange to Him because He is the creator of all things. He is the one that can give and take. He is the one that can judge and condemn us all. He is the only one that has the whole world in His hands. He is the only one that can do what He wants whenever He wants; there will not be any consequences because He is the perfect one. We must be proud to serve a great God like Him.

He is the only one that can say come to me as you are. People will judge the way you are, but Jesus Christ will not. When you come to Jesus Christ as you are; He will change you, and when Jesus Christ changes you, He does not make a little change in your life, He makes, a big change in your life, like He did for me.

We must stop talking about other people that we think that need to change because none of us are perfect, we all need to change something that is not right in us. All of us are sinners, it was not only King David with Bathsheba, or Adam and Eve, or the adulteress lady that they took to Jesus Christ who found mercy in Jesus Christ' eyes because of the sinners that were ready to stone her. All of us have a moment of weakness, it does not have to be adultery or stealing something and killing someone.

We just need to stay humble, obedient, and faithful to God until the day we die because the plan is to die in the Lord's arms. They might not see a smile on our face, but we know dying in God's arms will be a happy death, and that is how we must go to His Kingdom. The crown will belong to those who persevere until the end of their lives. True Christians will not want to go to hell, but the existence of hell is okay because if there was not a place called hell there would be no judgement or punishment. We would not have the freedom to choose if we must faithfully and sincerely serve God or if we will continue to be a whitewashed wall to go to hell.

MY HOPE TO HEAVEN

In the year of 2021, it was nighttime. I went to bed, and I had the best dream ever! I woke up happy, but after one or two second, I was angry at myself because I stood up close to a wall where I was praying. While I was praying, I felt like there was an army that came into the church. The army was marching inside the church, and I heard their boots getting louder.

I was worried, but I kept on praying harder, I did not move from where I was, and I did not turn my head to see if they were close to the room that I was praying in. That was a small church. It looked like my church members did not have a clue of the army that was marching in the church. I heard them talking to each other, laughing to each other, and the children were running around like always. There were parents that called their kids to go to kids' class for rehearsal.

The committee members were about to meet, and the children's class was having lunch. The youth class had a choral practice that day. And the others that did not go home yet sat at the tables to eat and talk to one another while the army's marching sound was still going on right in the church.

I did not think that any of them heard the marching army in the church. I prayed before I heard their boots like danger coming, and then I prayed stronger and harder. It was only me in that little church, I did not stop what I was doing to see what was going on. The same way I bowed my head and humbled myself in front of God with my eyes closed; I stayed that way and continued praying.

I did not turn my head to the right nor to the left. I did not leave the chapel that I was praying in to seek help from a human being like me. I knew the help would not come from no one other than whom I was praying; that was Jesus Christ. That is why I stood my ground, I did not freak out, and I stayed still. Because to me the army marching sound I have heard came to destroy us and the Temple.

People were still talking to their friends and families; children were playing to each other. There were a group of members that were going to missionary visits that day after they had done eaten. There were a group of members that served the church members and visitors food to eat before they went home or to missionary visits. They just sat down to eat at the tables.

MY HOPE TO HEAVEN

There were church members that helped bagging fruits and vegetables to give to members and visitors that were going home or to missionary visits that day. I had heard everything that was going on that day, but I did not hear anyone say anything about the army marching boots sound that was still going on. That sound was there, even when all those activities were going. No other church members were aware of it. I was still praying because I did not want to go out from that little church to the big church to see the youth choral practice that I like to watch.

When I finally opened my eyes, I saw three angels. One was in front of me, one at my right side, and one at my left side. I looked up to see their faces, but I could not. I looked down to see if I could see their feet, but I could not. Because they were so tall they were like the very tall poles on the streets. The only things that I could see were the bottoms of the things that tied their waists.

The one at my right passed his or her left arm under my right arm to support my back. The one at my left passed his or her right arm under my left arm to support my back. The one that stood in front of me had passed His right arm under the left arm of the one at my left, and He passed His left arm under the right arm of the one at my right.

In my mind the one that was in front of me was Jesus Christ

because He was the only one that had a light on His face that was shining down on me and blurred my vision. When I looked up, I thought that I could see His face. O the Lord knew that I was determined to see His face and the other angels, but it was nice trying. I tried to look down again to see their feet, which did not happen. I was so, so happy even though I could not see His face. I knew that was my Lord and Savior Jesus Christ that came to pick me up with the other two angels.

They started to be ascending with me, the roof top of the church did not open or move we were going up. At that time, the sound of the marching army was still going on. I heard members talking to members right in the church, there were members that were in their cars, there were members in the parking lot. Nobody saw us going up. I looked down to see if they could see me, but we went so high that when I looked at them, they looked like ants, until I could not see them anymore. At that time, I thought I was leaving the earth for good and forever.

MY HOPE TO HEAVEN

I was having a blessing, I was so happy I thought I was finished with trials and troubles in this world that I lived in. I did not know what to say any more than "thank the Almighty God." Since I started ascended with them, I stopped praying, and when I looked down, I saw the clouds. I still could not explain that feeling. One thing that I had on my mind when I was ascending with the angels was why I could see the church members down there, and they could not see me nor hear the army sound that was still there when the angels ascended with me.

Because I was so happy when the angels ascended with me, I woke up from that dream I had with a big smile on my face. After one second, I was so angry when I realized that I was still on this earth, in this chaotic world. I felt so bad when I woke up in that dream. Because I felt at peace under the angels' wings. There was a cool breeze when they flapped their wings. Nothing better than that breeze, even the air conditioning cannot compare to that breeze.

I missed the moment that I have had in that dream, but I know one day, if I am still alive at the time of the second coming of Jesus Christ, it will not be a dream, but it will be a reality where I will see myself and other Christians with Him going to heaven for eternal life. Let us continue our faithfulness to follow Christ, give glory to Him, listen to

His voice, and respond to what He wants us to do.

The God of Abraham, Isaac, and Jacob knows that He gives me freedom from bondage, I am not dealing with anything that has nothing to do with God. I am not dealing with anything that can cause me loss. God knows that nobody is perfect, but I always ask Him to cover me and my children under His wings. To keep me and my family in church, to continue to have great relationship with Him to the end.

From where I was, to where I am now! There is nothing that can make me go back to the mess I was. No one can tell me where I was. I knew it because I had been there. I thank God that I do not have to deal with the devil anymore in my life, I do not have to save my money to waste for idols anymore. That was dirty, I was dirty and disrespectful to God. I did not know that He did not want anyone to serve other gods. I did not know that I was doing anything wrong until I went to that revival. I asked God for forgiveness; I repented of my sins, and I was born again.

I know I am a sinner; but idols are my worst enemies.

LET DOWN OUR PRIDE

Christians that do not grow spiritually are pridefully trapped. We must let down our pride to open our hearts, our minds, and souls to serve the Lord. Because if our minds are filled with clutter, we will not think right. There will be pride in everything we do. We are not supposed to let our mind and soul get trapped by regret. I do not say we cannot regret what we did that was wrong. If we apologize for what we did and ask God for forgiveness, we can move on without regrets.

As believers we cannot resent anyone, we do not have to do things by tradition that is a trap because time change, people change every single day, things change, and situations change. The same way we must change things that can bring sadness to the Holy Spirit. We need to let God to be in control of our lives.

Then we will remember everything He has done through us and for us. We will be surprised to see how blessed we will be. Just put in mind we will have to climb mountains, and He will be there with us, we will not be alone as He promises us. He is a promise keeper.

We must serve God diligently because God is a rewarder of Christians that serve Him diligently. And we must try to get closer to God every single day, the closer we get to God the lesser we will sin. True, we should not be afraid of nothing except of sin; yet we really need to be afraid of sin because it is what separates us from the Almighty God.

As Christ followers we should be grateful for God's love because no matter what we do wrong He loves us anyway. Every day we wake up with a gift that we do not deserve; that is the gift of grace. That is true love, and true love is God Himself.

Do not forget that we must do our best to be faithful to God. Like I said before we cannot call ourselves Christians while wasting time in church. We need to be in it sincerely because God does not pay for the Christians race beginner, but He pays for finishing the Christianity race. Which means dying with the resurrection germ in us, dying in God's arms. If there are believers that did not know that God does not like when we are using pride instead of humbling ourselves in front of Him. James 4:6 says, "God opposes the proud but shows favor to the humble."

LET DOWN OUR PRIDE

I am so grateful because by God's freedom I am free from bondage, I am free from idols, and I am free from the devil's slavery. I thank God even more! Because before He freed me, He took the slavery out of me. I did not see that coming, because I did not know that I was going to be a Jesus Christ follower today. I thank my Shepherd because He makes me one of His sheep, amen. Yes, He gave me the strength to respond to His calling when He had called me in that dream that night.

After I accepted Him, I remembered I had asked Him to give me courage and strength to serve Him sincerely and faithfully.

We must pray to the Lord our God fervently with an open mind and no confusion. Yes, nobody is perfect, but we know what we really want if we are not a whitewashed wall! We will do our best to serve God right.

All believers know our goal is to go to heaven; we must make prayer our best friend and keep on calling on the Lord our God. Do not stop seeking His face and His attentions, do not stop giving Him glory, be always humble to Him, and be a good listener to His voice.

Call to me and I will answer you, and will tell you great and hidden things that you have not known.

–Jeremiah 33:3

As Christians the worst place that we can be at is in the outside of God's will. Remember to always put God in everything that we think we might want to do. Whatever it will be do not forget to ask God if it His will to do this or to do that, He wants to be our Father and friend. So let Him know, He already knows everything that we are about to do, but He wants us to go to Him for every little thing, not only when we have problems like trials and temptations.

We must remember to preach the gospel of Jesus Christ, which is a command and a calling to us. God never forgot His responsibility toward us; we must be Godlike to take the gospel to every nation. To do that we must pray fervently because the devil will do everything in his power to make us think that we are tired, we are not clean enough, we do not have time for that now, we will do that later. We all know that we will not be able to go all over the world to preach the gospel, but if we donate in some way the gospel will go where we will not go. Now remember that Jesus Christ is coming soon. We do not know when; but do what we must do to be there with the saints. Do not let waste of time pass us by.

THE THREE ANGELS' MESSAGES

Then I saw another angel flying directly overhead, with an eternal gospel to proclaim to those who dwell on earth, to every nation and tribe and language and people. And he said with a loud voice, "Fear God and give him glory, because the hour of his judgment has come, and worship him who made heaven and earth, the sea and the springs of water."

Another angel, a second, followed, saying, "Fallen, fallen is Babylon the great, she who made all nations drink the wine of the passion of her sexual immorality."

And another angel, a third, followed them, saying with a loud voice, "If anyone worships the beast and its image and receives a mark on his forehead or on his hand, he also will drink the wine of God's wrath, poured full strength into the cup of his anger, and he will be tormented with fire and sulfur in the presence of the holy angels and in the presence of the Lamb. And the smoke of their torment goes up forever and ever, and they have no rest, day or night, these worshipers of the beast and its image, and whoever receives the mark of its name."

–Revelation 14:6-11

Babylon is more than ever in church nowadays, what used to be in the world is going on in the church. When we are doing what we are not supposed to do as Christians, that is living the Babylon life. When one foot, one hand, one eye in the church and the others are in the world we are living the Babylon life with a Christian's identity.

When we are doing the same things as the unbelievers, we are also living the Babylon life. I do not say all Christians are living the Babylon life, but there are Christians that do not know where they are standing at, that is the Babylon life because they do not put their trust in the Lord. They are going to church too, because that is where their parents used to take them, so they continue to go there.

When I say what is supposed to be going on in the world is now going on in the church, I am not talking about the temple. I am talking about us because we, Christians, are the church.

THE THREE ANGELS' MESSAGES

When we use the Christian identity to define ourselves, we must show people what being a Christian means. What I mean is, we must show the unbelievers the way a Christian should be in real life.

I said real life because there are people that are playing Christians, but they are not real Christians. For example: when they are at home, at work, or at any social gathering they are different people from who they are at church. That is the same thing as living a double life.

When Christians are living a double life, they are living the Babylon life. When calling themselves Christian and messing with their church members while married or engaged or already have a girlfriend or a boyfriend, that is living the Babylon life.

Anything we should not be doing as Christians that is forbidden by God are things that can drive or push us into the Babylon life. Instead of staying away from them, they are using them, and taking them to church with them anyway, even though they know that is not right in the eyes of God. But is it okay for them to still be living that Babylon life?

We can see they do not worry about the judgement that all of us must go through. They do not care about God's wrath, and they do not worry about their spiritual lives. As Christians, our first obligation is our spiritual lives, because without that there is no way we can have a great relationship with the Lord our Savior.

As we all know there are unbelievers that say they are spiritual because they are meditating by the waters or by the sea. There is an enormous difference, between us and them; because our spiritual lives come from the strength of Jesus of Nazareth and meditating the word of God, and that is what Christ followers must to do.

And we must remember, we should always walk saved because no one knows when we are going out or if we will be coming back home. So, walking saved is something we must work on, and the time is now!

THE THREE ANGELS' MESSAGES

It is true when a believer says goodbye to this life, heaven says hello to that believer. We as Christians, we must make the effort to be with the believers that the heaven will say hello to when we leave this earth.

And for the heaven to say hello to us we will have to work extremely hard for that to happen, by asking God to give us the strength to stay faithful to Him so we can always avoid the Babylon life.

We must realize there is an hour of judgement at hand. The judgement day is coming, nobody knows when; the best we as Christians must do is to prepare ourselves for that day. We need to do our best to keep on making things right with God, so Jesus Christ does not say He did not know us.

To be ready is now. There is no such thing as we will have time or be available for repentance. No one knows what is going to happen tomorrow, and tomorrow is not promising, so the time to repent ourselves to be there with the saints is now! To be ready for the second coming of Christ.

Newness starts now!

> *Create in me a clean heart, O God; and renew a right spirit within me. Cast me not away from thy presence; And take not thy Holy Spirit from me. Restore unto me the joy*

of Your salvation; and uphold me with Your free Spirit. Then will I teach transgressors Your ways; and sinners shall convert to You. Deliver me from blood guiltiness, O God, my tongue shall sing aloud of Your righteousness.

–Psalm 51:10-14

Repent, for the kingdom of heaven is at hand.

–Matthew 3:2

Therefore keep watching, because you do not know on what day our Lord will come.

–Matthew 24:42.

Then the kingdom of heaven will be like ten virgins who took their lamps[a] and went to meet the bridegroom. Five of them were foolish, and five were wise. For when the foolish took their lamps, they took no oil with them, but the wise took flasks of oil with their lamps. As the bridegroom was delayed, they all became drowsy and slept. But at midnight there was a cry, "Here is the bridegroom! Come out to meet him." Then all those virgins rose and trimmed their lamps. And the foolish said to the wise, "Give us some of your oil, for our lamps are going out." But the wise answered, saying, "Since there will not be enough for us and for you, go rather to the dealers and buy for yourselves." And while they were going to buy, the bridegroom came, and those who were ready went in with him to the marriage feast, and the door was shut. Afterward the other virgins came also, saying, "Lord, lord, open to us." But he answered, "Truly, I say to you, I do not know you." Watch therefore, for you know neither the day nor the hour.

–Matthew 25:1-13

GOD'S GOODNESS

The goodness of God is incomparable, no matter what we do, He always loves us the way He did before. He never changes, He wants us to realize when we are wrong, to have the courage to ask Him for forgiveness.

Once we are ready to ask for forgiveness, He will be here like always to forgive us because He is a forgiving God. Forgiving us does not mean that we are not going to pay for that sin. We will pay the consequences of that sin. Now! We must remember that we are not God, we cannot make people pay the consequences of their sins, but we can forgive and forget what they had done to us.

I know it is not easy for everyone to forgive and forget what people have done wrong in our lives. No matter if they were family or friends; we must forgive them. If we cannot do that by us, we can ask God to give us the courage to forgive and forget.

No matter if there were scars or wounds caused from those pains we still must ask God to help us forgive them. We cannot keep on going back to what happened. Usually, people forget the past because there was no scar to keep on reminding them what happened and where that happened.

You can forgive whoever used to hurt you, but when you look at the scar on your body you will remember who did that to you. The same way the Lord loves us enough to forgive us for anything we did wrong. We must do the same for whomever hurts us.

We cannot call ourselves Christians while we do not practice what Jesus wants us to do. We must forgive people so God can forgive us when we ask Him to please do so. We must learn to have compassion for others. I am sure we will want people to have compassion for us or to forgive us sometimes. We must do for others what we are expecting them to do for us.

I know that God's goodness cannot be replaced but we can try to be good to people even if they do not like or love us. We cannot choose people that we like or love to help. We must help everyone without exceptions, no matter what their color, race, or nationalities. And remember! We must like and love everybody as Christ loves everyone on this earth. We do not have to fall in love with them to love them.

GOD'S GOODNESS

When we think about goodness of God, we look at everything that God has created for us before He even created our first parents. He renews our lives every day. He is watching over us while we are sleeping. He stays behind the wheels for us. We went to work; our kids went to school. And we all came back home safe unharmed. That is God's grace right there, we do not deserve that, but by His grace, by His love and compassion, He forgives us.

If it was not for His goodness, we wouldn't be here today; we already know we do not deserve all that God has done and continues doing for us. We must do the same thing for other people that hurt us. We must act the same way God's acting towards us. We are not better than the ones that hurt us.

There is no one righteous, not even one; there is no one who seeks God. All have turned away, they have together become worthless; there is no one who does good, not even one.
–Romans 3:10-12

If we take our time thinking about people that hurt us, we will waste our time, because that will not take us anywhere. We must try to forget whatever pain that may cause the anger we might have towards people who hurt us. We should help them and stand by them if they are in need.

Like God does towards us, He never let go of us.

If we were God, no one we do not like or want would be here today; same here for us, we would not be here either you or me. We must remember whatever we do for someone we do it for the Lord not for us. We must do things for unbelievers and believers because that is what God wants. He does not choose and pick who to love and who to help. We must act God-like because that is the way as Christians we must be.

We must remove or erase whatever grudges and hatred we might have against anyone; we must let those habits go because those bad energies can get us sick. No matter what we had done wrong God never gave up on us. We should not give up on anybody. Because we must be Christlike, that will be best for us in God's eyes. If we need to have a clean heart to serve the Lord! We must start to forgive and forget today! Because we do not deserve the grace, mercy, forgiveness, and love that we always have from the Almighty God.

PRISON MINISTRY OR EVANGELIST

Remember, our job is to preach the gospel all over the world. Then will come the end of all things and it will be time for the second coming of Jesus Christ. While we have that job to do, we must remember to visit the offenders because they need to get the message too. We all know that wrongdoing can cause people end up in jail, but that does not mean we have to forget them.

It does not matter if we know them or not. It is our responsibility to take the gospel to them too. Who knows, they might have gone to church with their parents, they might think they know about Jesus. We must go tell them that Jesus loves them no matter what they did. They need to know there is someone that died for them.

And that someone is Jesus Christ, we must tell them that Jesus Christ is the only one that can set their lives straight. The message should concentrate on Jesus Christ our Savior. Sometimes friends and families forget about them. But we as Jesus Christ's followers, we cannot forget them. Because there are offenders that come from a broken family, there are offenders that come from dysfunctional families.

There are offenders that never heard someone say they love them as a mom or a dad, they never hear the words "I love you" from any family members. We must go tell them that God loves us so much, that is why He sent His only begotten Son to die for us all.

One week after I was born again, I felt like I had an urge to go preach the gospel in jail. I had not read the Bible cover to cover yet. I did not know what Jesus Christ said about visiting prisoners and the sick people. I was eager to do that one day, so I went to the prison and asked questions about that. I asked a corrections officer what I needed to do so my church could come to minister in that place.

The officer said they had all denominations there, but they could not have one denomination twice. He said if a denomination removed itself, that denomination could be replaced by that same denomination. For example: they already had a Baptist church there; they could not add another Baptist church there. They wanted to have one of each denomination. I went there many times to see if there was a vacancy for my church. I have never had that chance; I never gave up hope because I knew that idea was not mine it was the Holy Spirit's idea. Who was I to think that way?

PRISON MINISTRY OR EVANGELIST

When we visit the offenders, we must let them know that Jesus is the only hope for the world. He is the only one that can make them whole again if they think they are not. We have a job to do, we must do it right. God knows the angels can do it better than us, but He sent us anyway just to show us to learn to be responsible.

Like I said, we must concentrate on Jesus of Nazareth, if they want to challenge us be patient with them. Just tell them let see what the Bible says about that. We need to make sure that we are ready to show them what we are talking about is in the Bible. Because we never know they might ask us where we get what we just said, so, we can prove it.

Prison is a foreign land. Imagine yourself in a foreign land. Our visit is not to ask them why they are there. Let them mention that if they want to open to us. It is not our goal to take anyone's pain away. That is Jesus Christ's work to do, we cannot be the messiah complex. We need to help them deal with the word forgiveness so they can forgive themselves.

We need to sympathize; we need to be patient so we can be more Christ-like. Tell them it is okay to be depressed, but they cannot stay depressed forever. As we all know there are offenders in death row, they might say that they are innocent. The only thing we can do is listen to them and offer them Jesus Christ. Because He is the only one that can change things, we cannot help in these situations. If one of the offenders asks one of us to be there at the time of his or her execution, we can choose to say yes or no. If we say yes, we need to make sure we keep our promise to be there. Never make promises we cannot keep.

We must watch our language; we cannot refer to them as "folks" or "you people" in prison ministry. Remember our goal is to bring people to the bridegroom; we must preach for a cause not for laughter or applause. We must teach the offenders to become Jesus Christ's disciples. All of us born again are preachers and ministers.

> *For I was hungry, and you gave me something to eat, I was thirsty, and you gave me something to drink. I was a stranger and you invited me in, I needed clothes, and you clothed me, I was sick, and you looked after me, I was in prison, and you came to visit me.*
> **–Matthew 25:35-36.**

We must visit the sick too.

WHERE ARE WE SPIRITUALLY?

We cannot set the course for where we are going until we know where we are spiritually. We cannot say that we think we will be there, we must know if we going to be there or not. I do not know about you, but I know that I will be the first one to go to heaven.

If every born again says he or she will be the first one to go to heaven, every Christian on this planet will go to heaven. We do not need anyone to tell us where we are spiritually, but Jesus Christ knows where we are spiritually, and He's the only one that knows what is going on in everyone's life. We cannot lie to Him; we cannot hide anything from Him, because of His Omnipresence He knows and sees it all. 1 Peter 2:9: "But you are a chosen race, a royal priesthood, a holy nation, a people for his own possession, that you may proclaim the excellencies of him who called you out of darkness into his marvelous light."

We are adult men and women; we know what we want and what we like. It is true nobody can think for us, but we can watch for each other. If we see something, we must say something. If we realize there is something wrong, of course we will talk about it because we are siblings in Christ; we must support each other instead of criticizing each other.

If we cannot help our siblings in Christ by talking to them, we can pray for them so Jesus Christ can open their eyes if they want to stop messing with their spiritual lives. I said if they want to because God gives free will to everyone and they can choose if they want to follow the Lord with a clean heart or if they will choose to stay where they are to go to hell.

God's plan is for everyone on earth to go to heaven. We must change our ways now! Because we cannot use the Christian title for showing off but to make disciples for the Lord. We must practice what we are saying. We call ourselves Christ followers, but we all know if we do not fully surrender ourselves to God the Son, God the Father, God the Holy Spirit, we are wasting our time. That is why we must stop now! Whatever we know that can cause our loss.

Our Christianity must start at home. Any bad manners that cause a broken family must stop now! We need to stop being a white thumb filled with bones while in church we act like angels. We must stop making people happy in church to gain fans.

WHERE ARE WE SPIRITUALLY?

Tell them the truth. That is why they are there, to hear the truth. It is time to cut the chains: chains of abusing, mentally, physically, and verbally. It is time to cut the chains of cigarettes. It is time to cut the chains pulling to the wrong directions. It is time to cut the chains of drugs. It is time to cut the chains of brain washing. It is time to cut the chains of abuse. It is time to cut the chains of alcohol. It is time to cut the chains of cheating. It is time to cut the chains of distrust. It is time to cut the chains of the unfaithful to God and in your relationship. It is time to cut the chains of causing trouble. And it is time to cut the chains of causing pain to others. It is time to cut the chains of plan B. Because Jesus Christ did not leave His Kingdom to come to die for us to have a plan B. Plan B does not exist for true Christ followers because plan B is one foot in church, one foot in the world.

As we all know, the reason for death is sin, and the reason for sin is death. We must hate sin; we need to make sure that we watch carefully how we do things and how we word things because there will be consequences that we will not be able to skip. The biggest regret we can have is dying without Jesus Christ, but if we know and have Jesus Christ, our last breath on earth will be our first breath in heaven. To experience what I just said, we must ask Jesus Christ to continue to help us stay in His arms and continue to hide us under His wings. So, we must die with the resurrection germ in us. We must stay faithful to the Lord our Savior to die with His resurrection germ. We must make prayer our best friend to keep our spiritual lives alive. We do not want to be in church and not go to heaven. God's plan is for us to be with Him eternally, but it is up to us, because of that free will He gives us. It depends on us to choose where we want to go.

Like I said before, I do not know about you, but I know from where I was to where I am now! There is nothing in this world that can hold me back anymore, to not see God's face in heaven. In 2015, I was born again, and that was it for me. I really did not know why I was blind that way, but now I see. By the grace of the God of Abraham, Isaac, and Jacob, I am free from worshipping idols. Who the Son set free is free indeed. I am finished with this world until the day I will die. It is true I am living in this world, but I am not in the world. I am going to continue keeping my eyes on Jesus Christ my redeemer until my last breath on earth, which will be my first breath in heaven.

WHERE ARE WE SPIRITUALLY?

When we do not want to pray, we should be able to realize that is the devil trying to slowly kill our spiritual lives. The best thing to do is to cry aloud to God to ask Him for help and the strength that we need to pray Him sincerely and truthfully. If you feel like you are in church, but never encounter the Holy Spirit; something must be wrong.

Because people can give the message to us, but it is our choice to take it or not to take it. No one can force us to be born again. They can talk to you about it. That is the Holy Spirit's responsibility to make people give their lives to Jesus Christ.

Now! If you accept the Lord as your Savior, you must baptize by immersion to be born again; that is the best and especially important thing to do. It is true He says come as you are. He knows He is going to work on you if you let Him. You must clean your house so you can throw away everything you have in your closet and under your bed that you know God will not agree with. You must ask God to clean your heart and mind from clutters.

You must stop the bad habits that you have used when you were in the world. Anything that you used to do in the world is not for you anymore. Any bad spirit that you used to serve or deal with is not for you anymore. If it is not the Holy Spirit, it is not for you anymore. You must throw away all the bad manners, all the bad intentions, all the good luck charms, all the good luck coins and the good luck stones, the good luck bath. They are not true; that is what they put in people's minds. Today, you must know! Jesus of Nazareth is good luck because He says in Philippians 4:13, "I can do all things in Christ that strengthened me."

Even if you did not used to do all those things about which I was talking, you and God know there are things in your life that you need to throw away for you to serve Him better because nobody is perfect. When you become a Christian, you will be totally changed, and people will see the change in you because your lifestyle will change. You will not be the same as before, but you must stay in prayer so the devil does not find ways to make you do what he wants anymore.

WHERE ARE WE SPIRITUALLY?

We need to take note of how we feel and what we do not feel while we are in church. We cannot call ourselves Christians, which means Jesus Christ's followers, and not feel the presence of the Holy Spirit. As I said before we cannot go to church because our parents used to take us there, nor save place for other people that are in the world right now like I was.

Watch that nobody takes your place in church because the place I took is mine forever until the day the Lord will return. And people that are living in the world will come to take their place in church because we must continue doing the job that we are called to do. By doing so, people will come to church. Watch carefully for your place in church and keep your head and eyes straight at Jesus Christ. Only that is the key to your spiritual life.

Do not give up on God because He never gives up on us. He is steadfast. He always keeps His Word. We must keep our commitment with God seriously because the judgement that is coming for the world is real, and there will be people in church going for that judgement if we do not ask God to help us stay humble and faithful to Him by helping us push away all the bad ideas, all negative things that can stop us from going to heaven. When bad ideas coming to our heads, we give glory to the Almighty, pray, and then command the devil to stay away from us.

All God's followers must know and remember that the devil and his agents are real. And they are hiding behind all sins. James 4:7 says, "Resist the devil and he will flee from you." As we can see, we must push the devil away because if we do not push him away, we will waste our time because his plans is to drive our minds where we will not expect. Believe me, commanding the devil to stay away from us works.

Just ask God to give us the strength and power to do so. With His blood we can command any bad spirit to stay or go away. So, we can be free to serve the Lord. The decision is ours to take, no one can take if for us, because parents will not be able to save their kids, or their friends and children will not be able to save their parents in front of God's judgement because the salvation is personal.

Any decision to serve the Lord is today!

> *And if it is evil in your eyes to serve the Lord, choose this day whom you will serve, whether the gods your fathers served in the region beyond the River, or the gods of the Amorites in whose land you dwell. But as for me and my house, we will serve the Lord.*
>
> **–Joshua 24:15**

WHERE ARE WE SPIRITUALLY?

If there are things you need to stop doing, stop now! And if your eye causes you to stumble, pluck it out and throw it away from you. Matthew 18:9 says, "And if your eye causes you to sin, tear it out and throw it away. It is better for you to enter life with one eye than with two eyes to be thrown into the hell of fire."

We must decide to serve the Lord faithfully so we can go to heaven; that is the plan that God has for us as Christians. We cannot call ourselves believers while our hearts, our minds, and our souls are not truly surrendered to God. We must not look for nothing in this world because there is nothing in it that is good or going to be useful to us.

Whatever happens in our lives never to look back, let us keep going forward. We do not have time to waste anymore if some of us used to waste time. Remember we must be humble to God, look for His presence, always give Him glory in good times and in bad times. We must remember who we are, and our mission on earth. And as believers we need to keep our heads up to serve Him sincerely and faithfully for us to be able to make disciples for Him. I know only God the Father, God the Son, and God the Holy Spirit in trinity are perfect. But if we truly surrender our lives to Him to serve Him without doubts, we will serve Him right, by His strengths. Even nobody is perfect.

Do not forget what Jesus Christ's followers mean; we do not have to follow what people do to be their friends or popular like the world does. By following people right in the church, we can lose our souls. Always put that in mind, not everyone in the church is a true Christian. There are church members that are the devil's agents. They will do anything to take you to hell with them. If we do not have the Holy Spirit living in us, we will not have the spirit of discernment and we will not be able to recognize them.

Because we cannot judge anyone like they say do not judge a book by its cover, we need to always be in prayer and God will reveal them to us. The devil's agents are worse than the people that are doing bad things out there. Our eyes are focusing on the bad guys out there that we can avoid, but the devil's agents, if we are not spiritual in Christ, they will not be recognizable.

WHERE ARE WE SPIRITUALLY?

As believers we must be very vigilant to be spiritual.

> *Enter by the narrow gate. For the gate is wide and the way is easy that leads to destruction, and those who enter by it are many. For the gate is narrow and the way is hard that leads to life, and those who find it are few.*
>
> **–Matthew 7:13-14**

Not every Christian is seeking for more of God. We must seek God every single day in our lives. And we must show our kids to do the same so, they learn to lean on the Lord by trusting Him. We know when we are seeking God how powerful He is. That is why we want our kids to see the goodness of God. The kids can feel and see how seeking God can be.

They must know when we are seeking God, we are getting stronger, and we are getting everything we have been asking for if it is His will. When we are seeking His face, no one cannot stop us. We must show our children how to depend on God their Father. They need to know that God is looking for our attentions. So, they are making sure to learn to listen to God's voice.

We must train the children to learn how to pray and to be humble. They need to know how to keep a good relationship with Jesus Christ. When they are asking for things, we must tell them to pray about it. I want my kids to learn to trust the Lord in whatever situation to believe in God. Even if we can give them what they are asking for, we still need to show them how to be responsible for their actions so they know they are responsible to ask God to help their spiritual lives. And the best thing to do for them is to show them how to rely on God so they can trust God.

Our children must know that they cannot do anything without God the Father, God the Son, and God the Holy Spirit. They need to learn to ask God if it is His will to have this or that. Children that find things easily not usually understand and not listening to their parents. No matter if they are in the church or in the world. That is why we should show them to do not take things for granted. We must tell the kids to always consult God for anything they will have in mind. They need to know that Jesus Christ is the answer to everything, and He is the only hope for the whole world. The kids must know everything about how to serve the Lord sincerely and be faithful to Him until the end of time.

WHERE ARE WE SPIRITUALLY?

People can grow up in church, but they never know how to be true Christians. Growing up in church or growing up in a Christian family does not mean that you know how to be a Christian. Either your parent or someone else is supposed to be your mentor. Every born again needs a mentor. Each born again was supposed to have a mentor that will show them how to serve God and how to be humble to the Almighty God. They need to know how to ask God to give them strength to stay strong, to not give in, and to not give up. A mentor that will show them how be always in prayer so they can work on their spirituality.

As we all know, there is a big difference between people that are forced to accept Jesus Christ as their Savior, and people who were led by the Holy Spirit to be born again. It is very easy for the people that were forced to accept Christ to leave church because they were not ready, they did not open their hearts to accept Jesus Christ, they will not make any effort to read the Bible to learn about Jesus Christ and to stay in church.

However, the ones who were led by the Holy Spirit to be born again will stay in church because they knew they had found the truth; they will not need to look for anything else. No matter what happens to them they will stay in church. Whatever trials, challenges, or temptations, they will stay at the cross. These people open their hearts and souls to receive the Holy Spirit, they will not give in nor give up for anyone no matter what happens to them in church. We must stop thinking that we can do the Holy Spirit's work. Our responsibilities are to preach the gospel around the world and make disciples for the Lord, but it is the Holy Spirit's responsibility to work on people so they can be born again.

There was a blind man that heard there was going to be a revival in the street that he lived on. He had someone make two small boards for him with a shoelace attached to them. He hung them on his neck. One sign in front of his chest, the other sign on his back. It was like a long necklace that had two boards on it. That was a way to announce the revival. *Jesus is coming soon. There will be a revival starting this week at 7:00 pm at Salem Baptist church.* He just heard about it. He could not go there by himself, someone had to go with him because of his blindness. Until this day, they always say this man was the one that had sent more people to that revival.

FAMILY

Family started at Eden's garden with our first parents, Adam and Eve. Since the beginning the devil did not like the fact that God created family. The devil tried to create confusion between Adam and Eve. We know already families are Mom, Dad, and children. I am talking about actual blood related family. We must think that the children are watching every move their parents make, they might not say anything, that does not mean they are not watching. They are paying close attention to whatever we are doing as parents. We need to take time to listen to them and be ready to answer questions.

As we all know, man should leave his mom and his dad to go live with his wife. Even though, there are parents that do not prepare their children for that purpose if it is mommy and daddy that do everything around the house. We must teach our kids about God and show them how to help themselves, so they are not suffering when we are not around them. There are children that do not want anyone to show them anything they will try doing things around the house, there are children that will ask if help is needed, but there are kids that will not say or do anything until their parents give them chores to do, otherwise they will not get it.

Sometimes when kids easily get what they want or like from their parents, they do not want to pray nor go to church, and that is what the devil is waiting for, do not let him get what he wants. Because we love our kids, this does not mean we have to let them grow up without family education. We must remember we are not going to be around for them all their lives. Family is not only about the kids. We need to think about doing things for us that is for the family: mom, dad, and children.

We must show our kids to have love for God and to learn to respect their elders. Show them to read their Bible so they can learn about God. There are fathers that make sure their children know how to do things around the house and to learned to be a handyperson. Those kids trained to be great husbands and dads for their families. We should look to have fun always, go hiking together, go on vacation together, go camping together, travel together with our kids. And to love each other, sacrifice for each other, sometimes we need to show how far our love can go because our hatred can go further than our love. Mom and Dad must show love to each other so the kids can show love to them. Who can give what they do not have?

FAMILY

Boys that are trained by their fathers to be a handyperson become great husbands for their wives and great dads for their children. They can step up to help their wives and children to have a great and a happy family. What people do not understand is, the devil can make it difficult for couples to survive the marriage. Because they did not receive the same family education, it can be hard to understand each other. Usually, communication and financial freedom are the main things that cause family separation or a broken home. If they do not know how to communicate to each other it will be an everyday problem.

When the marriage is built on the rock that is Jesus Christ, the devil will not have the power to create confusion between them nor to destroy that marriage. One of them can say, "Honey, we need to talk." And the other one answers, "What do you want to talk about?"

That is the devil's way to break family. Believers must be very smart and know the devil's game. Family is a special thing, which is why if you do not ready for family do not force yourself to have one because it takes a strong man and a strong woman with the strength of God to stay in a marriage. To stay in a marriage, you and your husband should have your eyes on God, and on Him only.

If the couple is always in prayer, if they are humble to

God, if they believe and trust God, that family will have a successful marriage. When one of them wants to talk the other one will be willing to listen. They usually say those who marry young are not durable as mature people; this is not when the marriage is under God's protection.

A family without Jesus Christ, any storm can break it at any time, the family will not survive: "Unless the Lord builds the house, the builders labor in vain" (Psalms 127:1). Family is so important. Before thinking about having one, the couple should agree to each other to go to God to ask Him if it is His choice for them to marry one another. Because sometimes hearts can lie, and what you see it is not often what you get. If that person thinks he or she is getting older, they must get married now. Love is patience, do not rush to a marriage that you think you are ready for but later will be too late to change your mind. After creating that family you will be stocked in it. Family needs love, patience, understanding, and unselfishness. Family must be ready to share with one another, and parents must show the kids how to share between them so, they can share with them later and share to others too.

FAMILY

Nobody goes to sleep and wakes up with a family. And no one can force anyone to have a family if that person does not choose to. There is no such thing as "was not ready to have a family." Before getting married you must know what you are signing for, and you must know what you are putting yourself in to. After creating a family, "I was not ready" will not have its place in your arguments because having a family to take care of is not a joke. That is why it is something that should be taken seriously.

Always put God first in your relationships; do not settle without God's voice, do not get married without putting God to work in that marriage. Asking the Lord to be the center of that marriage is necessary. Because when God is the head of a family, storms will not be able to wipe that family out because God is the one that has control over that family. Ask God if he or she is the one that He wants you to marry and to let you know and bless the marriage for you.

Like I said before, the devil does not like the word "marriage"; he does not like family. You must start praying before the wedding and pray harder for your family before kids are involved. When the family is complete, be ready to raise the kids in church, so they learn about God at home and in church. Pray for them so they stay in church until the end of their lives. Because the devil does not like to see teenagers in church.

Spouses not raised the same way did not receive the same family education; they will find it difficult to live together, but they keep on trying until they cannot try anymore. That is when the only solution will be getting a divorce. Otherwise, family is supposed to submit to one another out of reverence for Christ. Ephesians 5:22 says, "Wives submit yourselves to your own husband as you do to the Lord." Ephesians 5:23 says, "Husband is the head of the wife as Christ is the head of church. Now as the church submits to Christ, so also wives should submit to their husbands in everything." Ephesians 5:24 says, "Husbands love your wife, just as Christ loves the church and gave Himself up for her." Marriage that does not have God's support does not last as long as the spouses think it will. Great marriage is for two people who have pledged to serve God faithfully and to serve one another with patience and understanding.

LEARN TO SERVE OTHERS

We need to learn to serve others for us to say we are God's servants, because we serve God by serving others. If we cannot practice service and generosity to others, we cannot say that we are God's servant. If you want to be happy right now, help someone, because happiness does not come from sex, a degree, accounts, but by giving your focus on somebody else. This will bring joy and happiness to your heart. Remember that serving others means well to them. There are many things we can do to help others; give them your time, help them get to work, hep them enroll or apply for school, feed them. Take them to church, take them to appointments, or take them to apply for work.

Give them a place to stay if they have nowhere to go. If they need clothes help them, not with what you would not wear, but do it for the Lord. Do for them things you would want others to do for you. Remember to be God-like because God always gives us great things, and you must do the same for others.

We must act Christ-like when it comes to giving. Because giving is an act of joy. Especially if you do not give to show off but to help people who are in need. Feed people who are hungry, there are people that can be embarrassed. Ask for help if you think they might need help and ask them if they know that you can afford to help them. We cannot say we are Christ followers and not act like Him.

We should help in every way like Christ does for us every day. Helping is what we must do every day in our lives. We are not better than the people who are in need. God helps us so, we can help others. We should never discourage help because of ungrateful people that we had help before. Remember that we do not help people to expect nothing in return, but we help people because that is what we must do as Christians. It is not about whether we serve. It is about how others experience our service. They say, "When you know, you know." That is the same for when you are helping people; if we do not do it right, we will feel guilty. If we do it right, we will feel happy. Our conscience will not be tormenting us. We must pray to serve everyone without choosing who to serve, and we must sacrifice ourselves for others that is what Christ-like means.

LEARN TO SERVE OTHERS

We do not do anything good in God's eyes, but He forgives us all and helps us wake up every morning. He helps our families and friends. What a faithful God, which is how we must be faithful to Him. We know God is love, well we need to be God-like so we can love other people without falling in love with them to help them. Help them reach their goals because by helping them they will be able to provide for themselves, their parents, or their families.

It is better to show people how to fish than give them a fish every single day. Remember there are two kinds of people; one who takes and one who gives. Let us stop being the one to take and start being the one to give. We must show people that are in need that we can help now! No one knows how much you know until they know how much you care about them.

Help our enemies. When we help them, God the Almighty takes pleasures in our acts. He knows anything that we have done, right or wrong, He never lets us down, He always has that same love for us. We cannot give up on someone because we do not talk or have a friendship with that person and consider him or her as our enemy. That is where the word Christ-like must be applied.

We do not need to know anyone to help them. God does not choose who to help or why. No matter what we did wrong, when we are in trouble or when we do not know what to do or where to go, if we cry out to Jesus Christ for help, He always helps us. When we help our enemies, God takes notes of that, and our blessings will have no limit. We must do our absolute best to help others because that is what we should do, and we must help everyone.

If we try to help people who are not in need, what will that do for us? That is not called helping others but pleasing others. What will that do for us in front of God? If we help people who are in need, then we can say that we are helping others. And when we help somebody do it for the Lord, not for us nor for any reciprocity from anyone. We do not have to show people that we are helping others, just do it from our hearts, and we do not have to make mistreated people feel like they are losers. God creates us with His image, we all have two things in common. That is the one true God as our Creator and Father, and to have the eternal life.

Printed in the USA
CPSIA information can be obtained
at www.ICGtesting.com
LVHW021034021124
795374LV00009B/187